Book Synopsis

I0191941

"*Kingdom Decrees For Sustaining The Vision*" *is a manual designed to equip the vision carrier with revelation on how to pray, release, plow, and sustain in the destiny and calling of God on his or her life. It will assist you in learning how to govern the vision as a pure visionary, and how to lead in excellence and shift those who are called to help bring the vision to pass. Learn what to expect as a visionary, what God requires from your destiny and vision, the art with flowing with God in destiny and in your life's vision, how to conquer hindrances and obstacles to the vision, and intercession and warfare tactics for bringing the vision to pass. This book is sure to SHIFT you into towering in who you are in God and successfully achieving the calling and destiny upon your life.*

KINGDOM DECREES FOR SUSTAINING THE VISION MANUAL

TaquettaBaker@Kingdomshifters.com

(Website) Kingdomshifters.com

Connect with Taquetta via Facebook or YouTube

Copyright 2014 – Kingdom Shifters Ministries

Taquetta's Bio

Taquetta Baker is the founder of Kingdom Shifters Ministries (KSM). She has authored fourteen books and two decree CD's. Taquetta has a Master's Degree in Community Counseling with an emphasis on Marriage, Children and Family Counseling, a Bachelor's Degree in Psychology and Associates Degree in Business Administration. In addition, Taquetta has a Therapon Belief Therapist Certification from Therapon Institute and has 22 years of professional and Christian Counseling experience.

Taquetta is also gifted at empowering and assisting people with launching ministries, businesses and books and provides mentoring, counseling and vision casting through Kingdom Shifters Kingdom Wellness Program. Taquetta serves on the Board of Directors for New Day Community Ministries, Inc. of Muncie, IN. In October 2008, Taquetta graduated from the Eagles Dance Institute under Dr. Pamela Hardy and received her license in the area of liturgical dance. Before launching into her own ministry, Taquetta served at her previous church for 12 years. She was a prophet, pioneer and leader of Shekinah Expressions Dance Ministry, teacher, member of the presbytery board, and overseer of the Altar Workers Ministry. Taquetta receives mentoring and ministry covering from Bishop Jackie Green, Founder of JGM-National PrayerLife Institute (Phoenix, AZ), and was ordained as an Apostle on June 7, 2014.

Taquetta flows through the wells of warfare and worship and mantles an apostolic mandate of judging and establishing God's kingdom in people, ministries, communities, and regions. Taquetta travels in foreign missions and throughout the United States. She has mentored and established dance, altar workers, deliverance, and prophetic ministries. Taquetta ministers in the areas of fine arts, all manners of prayer, fivefold ministry, deliverance, healing, miracles, atmospheric worship, and empowers and train people in their destiny and life's vision.

Connect with Taquetta and KSM at kingdomshifters.com or via Facebook. For more information regarding Bishop Jackie Green at Jgmenternational.org.

TABLE OF CONTENTS

FOREWORD

Typically when we think of the word vision we immediately think of the eyes. The eyes are an important part of our vision, and is one of the gateways in which we experience, encounter, see, and receive from God. There is more to vision than just the eyes, with the eyes we perceive, but then after we have perceived it is our decision to put into action that which we have become aware of. Without the vision we are walking throughout life aimlessly, without purpose, without distinction, without will, without life and without production. We were created for better, we were created for relationship and communion with God, and through that, we were created for His good works. We learn from Genesis 1:28 that we were created and blessed to be fruitful and multiply. Life, fruit, and production were designed to be brought about through us from the beginning. Without walking in the vision and the destiny of God our ability to truly establish the purpose to which we have been created is substantially diminished. The author of this book is excellent in shifting us to the position to which each of us has been created. And not only in general, but individually in the unique and intricate designs of God on each of our lives. Understanding calling, destiny, and vision in clarity can be a trying thing to do, but this book provides useful tools and clear explanations on how to understand the concept and purpose to what each of those are, and then goes on to provide clear scriptural references and distinct revelation on how to operate in each of those.

This book is the blueprint, and map of how to not only walk in the vision, but how to write it, make it plain, birth it, release it, reclaim it, revive it, cleanse it, rest it, and more. I see it as an architectural masterpiece. This book is a hands on tool, not only has she written, but she has gone even deeper by cultivating, developing, and promoting the growth of each reader by decreeing and even giving tools, life experiences and pointers in each chapter. Throughout the book the author provides well-defined and straightforward decrees and prayers that help break you through, shift you, and cultivate what has been written and imparted into you. Although each chapter may not be easy to read, and may cause you to look at yourself, it builds you up in who you are, who you will be, and all that you have been called and designed to be and do throughout your destiny and life's vision. It provides you with the wisdom and mature approach on how to recognize the wiles of the enemy and then will cause you to rise in authority and control over your life to combat and demolish the hindrances and the obstacles sent against your destiny and vision. In some cases in our lives the devil may not be the only one battling against us. Spiritually many of us never think of the fact that we can actually be our worst enemy and the main hindrance in our ability to advance and walk in our destiny and life vision. We may be quick to blame the devil, or our friends and families, or those who speak against us, when really the main resistor could be at work within us. Enlightenment on this matter will cause the reader to self-reflect and truly gain freedom and the strength to conquer and tower in this area. This revelation is excellent and brings about deliverance and healing to all of its readers. This book is endless in revelation and provides many scriptures, revelation, and concepts that can lead you in further personal study, prayer and cultivation. The fruit is immediate, limitless, and has no boundaries!

Jesus is our greatest example of one who walked in destiny and life's vision flawlessly. His life's vision was centered on doing only what He saw the Father doing as He walked in destiny and vision. We are created in that very image and have that same ability and capacity living inside of us. We have to call it out of dormancy, and out of comatose, and command it to come alive within us such that we too can establish the destiny and vision that is on our lives. As His visionaries and ones called into destiny before the foundations of the world we are in the bloodline of Jesus Christ and have His DNA. He is the firstborn of all creation and He is the exact likeness of the unseen God, and we too can rise and put on this likeness and conquer and reign in vision and destiny with signs, wonders, and fruits following.

Blessings, Nina Cook of Muncie, IN

Taquetta's Spiritual Daughter & Armorbear

Knowing My Destiny & Life's Vision

This book will address both destiny and vision. Destiny and vision go hand and hand in fulfilling the call of God on our lives.

Dictionary.com defines *calling* as:

1. Vocation, profession, or trade, what is your calling?
2. To summon by or as if by divine command he felt called to the ministry.
3. To summon to an office, duty, etc.
4. To designate as something specified

Merriam-Webster's Dictionary defines *destiny* as:

1. What happens in the future, the things that someone or something will experience in the future
2. A power that is believed to control what happens in the future
3. Something to which a person or thing is destined, fortune
4. A predetermined course of events often held to be an irresistible power or agency
5. Synonyms see fate

Merriam-Webster's Dictionary defines *vision* as:

1. The ability to see, sight or eyesight
2. Something that you imagine, a picture that you see in your mind
3. Something that you see or dream, especially as part of a religious or supernfatural experience

4. Something seen in a dream, trance, or ecstasy, especially a supernatural appearance that conveys a revelation

My definition:
- *Calling* is what you are anointed or appointed to do
- *Destiny* is where were we are going in life
- *Vision* is the journey and plans our lives will take to operate in our calling and achieve destiny

There are countless scriptures that let us know that God calls, orchestrated a destiny, and equips us with a vision to achieve His will for our lives. Decree out the list of scriptures to release personal enlightenment over your destiny and life's vision:

Proverbs 19:21 - *Many plans are in a man's mind, but it is the Lord's purpose for him that will stand.*

Psalm 119:105 - *Your word is a lamp to my feet, and a light to my path.*

Psalms 139:13-17 - *For thou hast possessed my reins: thou hast covered me in my mother's womb. I will praise thee; for I am fearfully and wonderfully made: marvellous are thy works; and that my soul knoweth right well. My substance was not hid from thee, when I was made in secret, and curiously wrought in the lowest parts of the earth. Thine eyes did see my substance, yet being unperfect; and in thy book all my members were written, which in continuance were fashioned, when as yet there was none of them. How precious also are thy thoughts unto me, O God! How great is the sum of them!*

Jeremiah 29:11 - *For I know the thoughts that I think toward you, saith the LORD, thoughts of peace, and not of evil, to give you an expected end.*

Jeremiah 1:5 - *Before I formed thee in the belly I knew thee; and before thou camest forth out of the womb I sanctified thee, [and] I ordained thee a prophet unto the nations.*

Romans 12:2 - *And be not conformed to this world: but be ye transformed by the renewing of your mind, that ye may prove what [is] that good, and acceptable, and perfect, will of God.*

Romans 10:17 - *So then faith [cometh] by hearing, and hearing by the word of God.*

Romans 8:28-30 - *And we know that all things work together for good to them that love God, to them who are the called according to [his] purpose. For whom He foreknew, He also predestined to be conformed to the image of His Son, that He might be the firstborn among many brethren. Moreover whom He predestined, these He also called; whom He called, these He also justified; and whom He justified, these He also glorified.*
Isaiah 55:12 - *So you'll go out in joy, you'll be led into a whole and complete life. The mountains and hills will lead the parade,*

bursting with song. All the trees of the forest will join the procession, exuberant with applause.

Isaiah 61:1 - The Spirit of the Lord GOD [is] upon me; because the LORD hath anointed me to preach good tidings unto the meek; he hath sent me to bind up the brokenhearted, to proclaim liberty to the captives, and the opening of the prison to [them that are] bound;

Isaiah 58:11 - And the LORD shall guide thee continually, and satisfy thy soul in drought, and make fat thy bones: and thou shalt be like a watered garden, and like a spring of water, whose waters fail not.

Colossians 1:20 - And God purposed that through (by the service, the intervention of) Him [the Son] all things should be completely reconciled back to Himself, whether on earth or in heaven, as through Him, [the Father] made peace by means of the blood of His cross.

Ephesians 3:20 - Now to Him Who, by (in consequence of) the [action of His] power that is at work within us, is able to [carry out His purpose and] do superabundantly, far over and above all that we [dare] ask or think [infinitely beyond our highest prayers, desires, thoughts, hopes, or dreams].

Isaiah 14:24 - The Lord of hosts has sworn, saying, Surely, as I have thought and planned, so shall it come to pass, and as I have purposed, so shall it stand.

``*Ecclesiastes 3:1* -To everything there is a season, and a time for every matter or purpose under heaven.*

> *Ecclesiastes 3:11* - He has made everything beautiful in its time. He also has planted eternity in men's hearts and minds [a divinely implanted sense of a purpose working through the ages which nothing under the sun but God alone can satisfy], yet so that men cannot find out what God has done from the beginning to the end.

> *Ephesians 1:5* - For He foreordained us (destined us, planned in love for us) to be adopted (revealed) as His own children through Jesus Christ, in accordance with the purpose of His will [because it pleased Him and was His kind intent].

I Was Meant To Be Decree

I am not a happenstance, a mishap, a mistake, an afterthought, a bastard, a curse or any other lie, people or the enemy has spoken about me. No matter what was done in man's will, I am God's chosen, I was meant to be.

I am the very thoughts of God. I am the devised plan of God. I am destined for God's greatness.

I HAVE INTENTIONAL PURPOSE! I was designed to rattle this world. **I am God's kingdom uprising! I will productively execute the plan of my existence.**

I am gaining greater revelation even now that I was meant to be. I just am and command the world to yield and operate in agreement with me being a part of its existence, and its ability to effectively glorify God and His kingdom. **WORLD YIELD AS I PURSUE DESTINY!**

I SHIFT to loving that I was born and that there is a calling and vision for my life. No more do I reject what was meant to be. Take it up with my Father if you have a problem with me.

For you Lord God are my designer, the orchestrator of my being. I willingly receive your marvelous works. Your marvelous works, I will achieve.

I WAS MEANT TO BE!

25 Hindrances To Destiny!
That Stinking Devil Is A Liar!

These points are not to make anyone feel bad but to quicken our spirits to assert our God given authority to pursue God's calling, destiny and vision for our lives.

1. Many think they have nothing to offer life. Their own self-hatred kills or hinders the call, destiny and vision for their lives.
2. Many people know their calling but lack revelation for achieving destiny or fulfilling their life's vision. Seek God! He reveals His plans to His people.
3. Many operate in their calling but are unfulfilled because they sacrifice God's ordained plan for their lives to achieve destiny and their life's vision. They achieve destiny and their life's vision but they are unfulfilled because God is nowhere in the journey.
4. Many people know their calling yet choose fame over God's orchestrated plan and vision for their lives.
5. Many desire fame and fortune so they reject God's will for their lives. They cannot get pass and focus on pursuing the lusts of the flesh, the lust of the eyes, and the prides of life. This aborts who they were truly called to be as they get stuck in pursuing a path that is not of God.
6. Many look for a quick road to destiny and fulfilling the vision. This is a time stealer for really working the plan of God for our lives.

7. Many get stuck in parts of the journey and never reach complete fulfillment of destiny or a vision.

8. Many just never get started. Many fear change. Many marry routine.

9. Many do not realize that their vision is generational and that they must connect with and impart into the next generation in order for their destiny to be fulfilled.

10. Many are too busy coveting and counterfeiting someone else's life to pursue their own calling, destiny and life's vision. They do not see the authentic value in simply being themselves.

11. Many do not like God's plan or method for their lives. They reject it because they want destiny and fulfillment their way. This is self-idolatry. When we reject ourselves, we reject God, as we are rejecting who He is in us.

12. Many share their vision with someone who steals the plan for themselves. They then give up because they do not realize that no one can ever be them. Even if someone steals it, they lack the authentic God pattern. It is just a counterfeit when it is stolen. It lacks you.

13. Many allow hurts - church hurts, leader hurts, job hurts, family hurts, childhood hurts, self-inflicted hurts and wounds to hinder the fulfillment of the calling on their lives. Reliving the pain and incidents, cycling in the pain and hurtful habits, self-hatred and self-sabotage, unforgiveness, anger, resentment, a desire for revenge, thwarts their calling, destiny and God's ordained vision.

14. Many are bound by generational curses of slavery, procrastination, stagnation, spiritual and natural murder and/or suicide. These are destiny killing strongholds.

15. Many are bound by ancient curses and rituals and do not realize that somebody in their lineage dabbled in idolatry and has sold everyone's destiny to the devil for power or gain. If you just cannot get ahead you might want to explore this option in prayer.

16. Many are bound by culture, family and cultural traditions and choose the poverty and displaced mentality of culture and family traditions over their calling. We call it being true to our peeps. Being true will cost you destiny.

17. Many have false loyalties and allegiances to people, family members, leaders, jobs, churches, and therefore, abort destiny.

18. Many received poor or destructive counsel and it hindered their destiny or life's vision. Please know that God is one of redemption and restoration. Seek him on renewing your vision and destiny.

19. Many just need wise counsel and Godly direction to SHIFT into operating in their calling, destiny, and God's ordained vision.

20. Many lack or have not aligned with effective connections, role models and mentors to assist with the calling, destiny and plan for their lives.

21. Many are rejected by those who are called by God to help them. Respect of persons can hinder one's destiny and vision.

22. Many have sought assistance, but some who have made it, will not share the secrets to their success. They tell you to work like they did or want to keep you working their vision rather than assisting you in prospering in who you are. There is no revelation of generational impartation, release or heritage.

23. Many are too prideful to ask for help.

24. Many have been given a mapped out plan by God and are just too lazy or fearful to go forth.

25. Many encounter demonic interference where the devil seeks to kill God's plans by any means necessary. These demonic attacks can cause destiny catastrophe and even physically kill a person or cause a person to kill or want to kill themselves. The lack of understanding that just as God has a plan for our lives, the devil also has a plan to kill it and us, causes many to be blindsided by the wiles of the enemy. Truly in this day and age, there is enough knowledge in this area for kids to be guarded and raised under Godly covering so that the enemy's plans are annihilated. Yet even many kids in Christian homes grow up unprotected from the devious plans of the enemy. And some children are in homes where they live with the destiny killer.

It is essential that we take control over our callings, destinies and life visions. This will bring true fulfillment to our lives but more importantly, enable God to get all the glory He deserves and requires out of our lives. Let us resist, reject, and annihilate these hindrances by submitting to the calling and vision on our lives.

James 7:8 - *Submit yourselves therefore to God. Resist the devil, and he will flee from you.*

1Peter 5:6 - *Humble yourselves, therefore, under God's mighty hand, that he may lift you up in due time.*

Romans 15:8 - *For whether we live, we live unto the Lord; and whether we die, we die unto the Lord: whether we live therefore, or die, we are the Lord's.*

Psalms 75:7 - *But God is the judge: he putteth down one, and setteth up another.*

1Samuel 2:7 - *The LORD sends poverty and wealth; he humbles and he exalts.*

3John 1:2 - *Beloved, I wish above all things that thou mayest prosper and be in health, even as thy soul prospereth.*

2Corinthians 1:20-22 - *For no matter how many promises God has made, they are "Yes" in Christ. And so through him the "Amen" is spoken by us to the glory of God. Now it is God who makes both us and you stand firm in Christ. He anointed us, set his seal of ownership on us, and put his Spirit in our hearts as a deposit, guaranteeing what is to come.*

Hebrew 6:11-13 - *We want each of you to show this same diligence to the very end, in order to make your hope sure. We do not want*

you to become lazy, but to imitate those who
through faith and patience inherit what has
been promised.

Isa 58:11 *- And the Lord shall guide thee*
continually, and satisfy thy soul in drought,
and make fat thy bones: and thou shalt be like a
watered garden, and like a spring of water,
whose waters fail not.

New Living Translation - The Lord will
guide you continually, giving you water
when you are dry and restoring your
strength. You will be like a well- watered
garden, like an ever- flowing spring.

Destiny Now!

There can be many obstacles to the vision, yet when we are children of God, obstacles are only stepping stones for God to get glory and for us to be continuously propelled forward into destiny!

> *1Corinthians 2:9-10 contends:*
> Eye hath not seen, nor ear heard, neither have entered into the heart of man, the things which God hath prepared for them that love him. But God hath revealed them unto us by his Spirit: for the Spirit searcheth all things, yea, the deep things of God.

Prepared in the Greek is *hetoimazo* and means:
1. To prepare, prepare, provide, make ready.
2. To make ready, prepare to make the necessary preparations, get everything ready
3. Metaphor:
   A. Drawn from the oriental custom of sending on before kings on their journeys persons to level the roads and make them passable
   B. To prepare the minds of men to give the Messiah a fit reception and secure his blessings

We see from this passage of scripture that though we may have obstacles and may not know what is ahead, God has prepared everything for us, His loved ones, to make every challenge passable. Whewwwwwww!

With that being said, it is time to get out of our own way and pursue or SHIFT higher into the visions that God has placed in our belly. Declare it with me, **"VISION COME FORTH - DESTINY NOW!"**

Destiny Now Decree

Lord right now we fall out of agreement with and cancel the lies that we there are too many obstacles to the vision. Even as you have created us and instilled great vision in us, you have also prepared everything along the way for us to achieve destiny and successes in every area of the visions within us.

We decree our mindsets are changing today regarding obstacles. We no longer look at them as roadblocks. We no longer allow them to dictate our ability to release and mature the visions you have granted to our hands.

We thank you even now for the glory you will receive from every obstacle. We thank you even now that every obstacle is catapulting us into being all the more successful, while unveiling the strength, will, and greatness of our destiny!

No more delay!

No more frustration!

No more stagnation!

No more hopelessness!

We activate ourselves in the vision and declare **"VISION COME FORTH - DESTINY NOW!"**

We thank you for every passage way you have created for us to conquer in our journey of releasing, cultivating, and maturing the vision.

Conquering Self-Sabotage
The Enemy Within

Though we have just learned from the first chapter that God has prepared a passable way to conquer every obstacle to the vision, it is one thing for others to attempt to sabotage the vision of God in our lives; it is a whole other matter when we hinder our own vision and destiny. I would contend that the biggest enemy to the vision is not just sabotage, but self-sabotage.

Dictionary.com defines *sabotage* as:
1. The act of destroying or damaging something deliberately so that it does not work correctly
2. Any underhand interference with production, work, etc., in a plant, factory, etc., as by enemy agents during wartime or by employees during a trade dispute.
3. Any undermining of a cause.

The challenge with self-sabotage is that a person becomes their own enemy. These self-inflicting behaviors and actions are not easily recognized as the person is usually operating from a wounded place, false loyalty or false perception. He or she continues to blame others for his or her actions or live from the delusional or worldly loyalty/perception and thus cannot receive, comprehend, or cultivate what God is saying for his or her life. The person is usually blaming the church, leaders, momma, daddy, teachers, neighbors, the job, hurtful experiences, lack of money, lack of guidance, lack of support, for the reason he or she has not pursued their dreams and visions. This person will continuously make excuses for the reason prospering forward is not an option and truly becomes his or her own destiny killer. Because the wound and hurtful situations are legit, and even the false reality the person has created out of fear, insecurity, false loyalty have become safe havens, the person continuously relives the pain and/or remains stagnant inside his or her delusion and allegiance, while blaming others and situations for the reason he or she cannot get ahead in life.

Moses is a decent example of one who operated in a spirit of self-sabotage. God had to continuously combat Moses' self-defeating thoughts of not wanting to be the leader that confronted Pharaoh, while leading the Israelites out of Egypt into the promise land.

> ### Exodus 3:11-14:
> And Moses said unto God, Who am I, that I should go unto Pharaoh, and that I should bring forth the children of Israel out of Egypt? And he said, Certainly I will be with thee; and this shall be a token unto thee, that I have sent thee: When thou hast brought forth the people out of Egypt, ye shall serve God upon this mountain. And Moses said unto God, Behold, when I come unto the children of Israel, and shall say unto them, The God of your fathers hath sent me unto you; and they shall say to me, What is his name? What shall I say unto them? And God said unto Moses, I Am that I Am: and he said, Thus shalt thou say unto the

17

children of Israel, I Am hath sent me unto you. And God said moreover unto Moses, Thus shalt thou say unto the children of Israel, The Lord God of your fathers, the God of Abraham, the God of Isaac, and the God of Jacob, hath sent me unto you: this is my name for ever, and this is my memorial unto all generations.

When reading chapter three of Exodus, we find Moses giving God all kinds of reasons he is not equipped for the vision at hand. Moses has had an unexplainable encounter with God through the burning bush. God has intricately shared the vision with Moses and giving him revelation of his calling and destiny. God has also revealed the keys to overcoming the obstacles and inadequacies Moses presents. Because Moses is operating from a worldly reality and from a wounded place of being abandoned as a child and seeing those that raised him make slaves out of his people (Exodus 2), he cannot discern or comprehend that the GREAT I AM is with him and has orchestrated this assignment for him. He only sees who he is not rather than who he really is and is supposed to be. This is the murderous fruit of self-sabotage. It is not outside forces that are hindering Moses it is the enemy within that defeats him.

I would go as far as to say that because Moses never received deliverance from self-sabotage, he was susceptible to participating in it. We see this in an error he made when the Israelites were in need of water and were complaining and murmuring. Moses became angry and struck the rock when God gave directions for him to speak to it. Even though

Moses is known as the deliverer of the Israelites, he himself did not take them into the promise land as he died right outside the promise land. He got to see a glimpse of the full vision and his life's destiny, but never partook of the rewards of it (Numbers 20:7-12, Deuteronomy 34:1-6).

Numbers 20:7-12:
And the Lord spake unto Moses, saying, Take the rod, and gather thou the assembly together, thou, and Aaron thy brother, and speak ye unto the rock before their eyes; and it shall give forth his water, and thou shalt bring forth to them water out of the rock: so thou shalt give the congregation and their beasts drink. And Moses took the rod from before the Lord, as he commanded him.

And Moses and Aaron gathered the congregation together before the rock, and he said unto them, Hear now, ye rebels; must we fetch you water out of this rock? And Moses lifted up his hand, and with his rod he smote the rock twice: and the water came out abundantly, and the congregation drank, and their beasts also. And the Lord spake unto Moses and Aaron, because ye believed me not, to sanctify me in the eyes of the children of Israel, therefore ye shall not bring this congregation into the land which I have given them.

Moses was subtly compliant to fulfilling the assignment of the Lord but he never entered the true obedience of surrendering His life and will to God. Moses never became the journey. He never

19

became destiny. He never became the vision. He never SHIFTED into really accepting that he was fit for the call on his life. He constantly needed reassurance and emotional provision to feel secure in doing what God had granted to his hands. At some point we have to release the insecurities and marry (covenant) with the vision and calling on our lives. Many spend so much time having God and others stroke their egos with constant prophecies and puffed up accolades until they do not SHIFT into really operating in the call and vision for their lives. This is self-sabotage. It is the enemy within, stealing our time, our destiny, our God ordained vision.

Another view of self-sabotage is Samson. Samson was a miracle baby. He was God's ordained Nazarite from birth. Samson carried the vision of delivering the Israelites from the oppression of the Philistines (*Judges 13-16*). A Nazarite is someone who vows to consecrate and separate themselves to be used for the glory of the Lord. In ancient times, they did not cut their hair, drink wine or defile themselves by the presence of a corpse. Samson knew he was called and set apart. He understood the vision he carried, he knew the secret to his strength, and he recognized what made him successful in fulfilling his God ordained vision. Yet despite being dedicated and raised in the presence of the Lord, cultivated in the calling and vision that was on his life, Samson had a propensity for the very thing he was born to destroy. Sampson partook of the Philistines ways and culture and then used his call and strength (God's ordained vision) to taunt, ridicule, enrage, and slaughter the

Philistines. In his partiality to the Philistine lifestyle, Samson haughtily made covenant with it, as he married a Philistine named Delilah. He now possessed within his loins, the enemy of self-sabotage.

Covenanting with self-sabotage caused Samson to be careless and mishandle his calling and God ordained vision. Unlike Moses, Samson knew his strength and potential. He allowed this self-awareness to drive and rule him. He was not yielded to the Nazarite calling and deliverance vision that was on his life. As we read the story of Samson, we find him revealing the secret of his strength to his wife Delilah and being overtaken by the Philistines.

> *Judges 16:16-21:*
> *And it came to pass, when she pressed him daily with her words, and urged him, so that his soul was vexed unto death; That he told her all his heart, and said unto her, There hath not come a razor upon mine head; for I have been a Nazarite unto God from my mother's womb: if I be shaven, then my strength will go from me, and I shall become weak, and be like any other man.*
>
> *And when Delilah saw that he had told her all his heart, she sent and called for the lords of the Philistines, saying, Come up this once, for he hath shewed me all his heart. Then the lords of the Philistines came up unto her, and brought money in their hand. And she made him sleep upon her knees; and she called for a man, and she caused him to shave off the seven locks of*

his head; and she began to afflict him, and his strength went from him.

And she said, The Philistines be upon thee, Samson. And he awoke out of his sleep, and said, I will go out as at other times before, and shake myself. And he wist not that the Lord was departed from him. But the Philistines took him, and put out his eyes, and brought him down to Gaza, and bound him with fetters of brass; and he did grind in the prison house.

One key we see here is when the Philistines had Samson in captivity, they gouged out his eyes - his vision so he could not see. The bible lets us know that without vision the people perish (Proverbs 29:19). With no natural vision and no supernatural strength, Samson had to SHIFT to operating in spiritual vision. He still knew he was born to deliver the Philistines. This was a spiritual vision he carried and operated in at times, but did not truly live a committed life to. He however, was graced with a moment of Godly redemption, where he could sacrifice his life to fulfill the calling that was on his life.

Verse 22-30:
Howbeit the hair of his head began to grow again after he was shaven. Then the lords of the Philistines gathered them together for to offer a great sacrifice unto Dagon their god, and to rejoice: for they said, our god hath delivered Samson our enemy into our hand. And when the people saw him, they praised their god: for they said, our god hath delivered into our hands our enemy, and the destroyer of our country,

which slew many of us. And it came to pass, when their hearts were merry, that they said, Call for Samson, that he may make us sport. And they called for Samson out of the prison house; and he made them sport: and they set him between the pillars.

And Samson said unto the lad that held him by the hand, suffer me that I may feel the pillars whereupon the house standeth, that I may lean upon them. Now the house was full of men and women; and all the lords of the Philistines were there; and there were upon the roof about three thousand men and women, that beheld while Samson made sport. And Samson called unto the Lord, and said, O Lord God, remember me, I pray thee, and strengthen me, I pray thee, only this once, O God, that I may be at once avenged of the Philistines for my two eyes.

And Samson took hold of the two middle pillars upon which the house stood, and on which it was borne up, of the one with his right hand, and of the other with his left. And Samson said, Let me die with the Philistines. And he bowed himself with all his might; and the house fell upon the lords, and upon all the people that were therein. So the dead which he slew at his death were more than they which he slew in his life.

Spiritual vision is key to the success of destiny. Moses and Samson never received the full rewards of the callings and visions upon their lives because they allowed natural vision to override spiritual vision. They got to operate in their calling at times and work the vision. They saw triumph and fruit along the way. But the ultimate voyage or passage way that obtained their full rewards was aborted because of self-sabotage.

- Many never get started because of sabotage
- Many start but quit because of self-sabotage
- Many fumble through destiny but they never reap the true rewards of destiny or the vision to which they have toiled all because of self-sabotage

It is important to be aware of this destiny/vision killer so we do not become our own enemy.

Moses characteristics of self-sabotage:
- Insecurity
- Inadequacy
- Self-defeating and undermining thoughts
- Anger
- Murder
- Wounds from being abandoned at birth and his people being slaves of those who raised him
- Not having God's revelation of the reason he was raised in Pharaoh's house
- Needing constant emotional encouragement that he was called to be a deliverer and conquer the promise land
- Did not have a revelation that this was a new chance at achieving destiny
- Feelings of being stuck, hopeless
- Settling and choosing loneliness and unhappiness when God was trying to SHIFT him into destiny fulfillment

- Does not feel worthy because of who he is and mistakes he has committed
- Runs away in the face of adversity
- Letting fear drive him rather than faith
- Caring too much about what others will think or what the enemy will do
- Lack of temperance and disobedience (allowed those he led to distract, discourage and anger him; became angry and struck rather than speak to the rock)
- Actions tend to cause negative consequences for others (Moses striking the rock caused Aaron not to enter the promise land because God had given them both the directions of speaking to the rock to bring forth the water - Numbers 20:24)

Samson's characteristics of self-sabotage:
- Lust
- Fornication
- Pride and haughtiness (only seeing his strength and power and not embracing or being open to explore and change his flaws)
- Carelessness
- Lived on the edge and took ungodly risks with his life and calling
- Drunkenness
- Married (made covenant) and partied with the idolatrous enemy
- Rebellion
- Strayed from his Godly upbringing
- Ignoring his gut and intuition not to share the truth with Delilah
- False allegiance to his Philistine wife which caused him to reveal the secret to his strength

- False reality that he could not be overpowered or overtaken
- Knew his destiny and calling but lacked drive and focus in pursuing it successfully
- Made excuses for his behaviors of rebellion and idolatry
- Did not listen to wise counsel and warnings from those in authority
- Put the Israelites at risk for slaughter as due to captivity he was no longer able to protect them
- Was only self-sacrificing to the vision when it benefited him or brought deliverance to him (when in captivity he was willing to die to avenge himself, God and the Israelites)

Deliverance and inner healing is needed to cleanse and uproot the toxins of self-sabotage. It is not just a spirit but the characteristics often intertwine in one's personality, making deliverance very difficult. Because self-sabotage operates like a covenant, a divorce and constant dejection and refusal to participate in the characteristics of sabotage is needed for true deliverance to occur. A person must be aware of what elements of self-sabotage operate in his or her personality so that the person can counterattack them with God's truth regarding his or her destiny and calling. Moreover a person's thoughts, will and action has to be in agreement with God's plan for his or her life so that when faced with sabotage, they will give no room to this enemy. Today we decree no more self-sabotage. We get out of our own way and SHIFT fully into the destiny and visions of God for our lives.

Divorcing Sabotage Decree

In the name of Jesus, we repent for allowing the spirit of sabotage into our lives. We fall out of agreement with this enemy and declare that we divorce it right now in Jesus name. We disengage from every tentacle and intertwining of its nature, character, thought pattern, thought processing, behavior, effect, and consequence. We say we no longer desire self-sabotage to be a part of our lives and command a mending to every split it has caused in our identity and personality. We decree singleness of heart and mind right now in the name of Jesus. We declare that we have the mind of Christ and we are being continuously transformed by the renewing of our mind and receive all Jesus' has for us.

We fall out of agreement with every other destructive call, plan and path. We fully marry, covenant wholeheartedly with, the call, destiny and vision of God for our lives. We command the eyes of our understanding to be enlightened to not only discern the call, vision and destiny for our lives, but to have constant clarity regarding our purpose and how God desires to get glory out of all He has ordained for us.

We say our lives are about you God. We sacrifice ourselves willingly and declare the fullness of **Romans 14:8** over our lives and lineages, *"For whether we live, we live unto the Lord; and whether we die, we die unto the Lord: whether we live therefore, or die, we are the Lord's."* We belong to you Lord and command a cultivation of your character and likeness in every existence of our being.

We thank you that your character and likeness will aide us in further combating self-sabotage, and that this obstacle is no longer a road block for us achieving destiny and bringing forth your ordained vision.

We say, **"Destiny Now!"** as we propel into successfully achieving your vision! In Jesus name it is so! Amen!

Kingdom Initiative - Christ Mindedness!

Most destinies and visions have nothing to do with what we have and do not have, who we know and do not know, who will and will not help us. Our dreams and visions are about our own willingness to really do what is necessary to pursue and achieve them.

Dictionary.com defines *initiative* as:
1. An introductory act or step, leading action
2. Readiness and ability in initiating action, enterprise
3. One's personal, responsible decision, to act on one's own initiative

Dictionary.com defines *Initiate* as:
1. To cause or facilitate the beginning of, set going
2. To induct into membership by or as if by special rites
3. To instruct in the rudiments or principles of something, introduce

God's visions are generationally focused and are for the good of His kingdom and all of mankind. We see this in *John 3:16*:

> *For God so loved the world, that he gave his only begotten Son, that whosoever believeth in him should not perish, but have everlasting life.*

People tend to have initiative for what they are passionate about or what benefits them. They

29

therefore, have a difficult time fully investing in the vision. There is also a mindset at times that since God ordained it or prophesied it, He is going to do it all, even the leg work. We assume the vision is going to miraculously appear. This is one of the challenges with prophecy, as in this day and age, prophecies tend to be blanketed statements such as "you are going to be great," with no direction or clarity. Many do not pray into what God is speaking. They are just waiting for the statements to come to pass, with no accountability on their part in destiny and/or the vision manifesting. Please know that the greatest of inventors and business owners, ministry visionaries had to take initiative. We are waiting on someone to help us, do it for us, and give us a chance. We are waiting on someone to ordain us, certify us, and give us that seal of approval. Sometimes, we are just plain lazy and do not want to do the leg work - dirty work. We must ascertain that destinies and callings produce successful visions through hard work and sacrifice.

Joseph's blanketed prophetic dreams regarding the destiny and vision on his life resulted in increased sibling hatred, rebuke by his father, being thrown into a pit and left for dead, and eventually sold into slavery.

> *Genesis 37:3-8:*
> *Now Israel loved Joseph more than all his children, because he was the son of his old age: and he made him a coat of many colours. And when his brethren saw that their father loved him more than all his brethren, they hated him, and could not speak peaceably unto him.*

And Joseph dreamed a dream, and he told it his brethren: and they hated him yet the more. And he said unto them, Hear, I pray you, this dream which I have dreamed: For, behold, we were binding sheaves in the field, and, lo, my sheaf arose, and also stood upright; and, behold, your sheaves stood round about, and made obeisance to my sheaf. And his brethren said to him, Shalt thou indeed reign over us? Or shalt thou indeed have dominion over us? And they hated him yet the more for his dreams, and for his words.

Verse 20-24:
Come now therefore, and let us slay him, and cast him into some pit, and we will say, some evil beast hath devoured him: and we shall see what will become of his dreams. And Reuben heard it, and he delivered him out of their hands; and said, Let us not kill him. And Reuben said unto them, Shed no blood, but cast him into this pit that is in the wilderness, and lay no hand upon him; that he might rid him out of their hands, to deliver him to his father again.

And it came to pass, when Joseph was come unto his brethren, that they stript Joseph out of his coat, his coat of many colours that was on him; and they took him, and cast him into a pit: and the pit was empty, there was no water in it.

I cannot truly say that Joseph really understood that such consequences would occur for simply sharing a prophetic dream. Yet the minute we begin to identify the calling and destiny on our lives, the enemy orchestrates his dirty work to destroy it. While we are idle and think our dream will

31

miraculously unfold, the enemy is orchestrating mass destruction to make sure we remain stagnant and unproductive.

Joseph's brother decided to fetch him out of the pit and sell him into slavery. As a slave, Joseph could have resisted his fate and did as less as possible to get just get by in life. He could have taken the mindset that he would just frolic through life and wait on his dream to manifest. Though Joseph did not know he was in alignment with destiny and the prophetic dream he had, he did not waste his time as a slave. He worked hard, gained favor of the guards and was eventually given charge over Potiphar's house and over all the other slaves. Joseph operated in kingdom initiative and it aligned him with destiny.

> *Genesis 39:2-6:*
> *And the Lord was with Joseph, and he was a prosperous man; and he was in the house of his master the Egyptian. And his master saw that the Lord was with him, and that the Lord made all that he did to prosper in his hand. And Joseph found grace in his sight, and he served him: and he made him overseer over his house, and all that he had he put into his hand. And it came to pass from the time that he had made him overseer in his house, and over all that he had, that the Lord blessed the Egyptian's house for Joseph's sake; and the blessing of the Lord was upon all that he had in the house, and in the field. And he left all that he had in Joseph's hand; and he knew not ought he had, save the bread which he did eat. And Joseph was a goodly person, and well favoured.*

Even Jesus purposed to operate in initiative. Jesus'
initiative was to do God's work and to please Him.

> ### John 8:28-29
> *Then said Jesus unto them, when ye have lifted
> up the Son of man, then shall ye know that I am
> he, and that I do nothing of myself; but as my
> Father hath taught me, I speak these things.
> And he that sent me is with me: the Father hath
> not left me alone; for I do always those things
> that please him.*
>
> ### The Amplified Version
> *So Jesus added, When you have lifted up the
> Son of Man [on the cross], you will realize
> (know, understand) that I am He [for Whom
> you look] and that I do nothing of Myself (of
> My own accord or on My own authority), but I
> say [exactly] what My Father has taught Me.
> And He Who sent Me is ever with Me; My
> Father has not left Me alone, for I always do
> what pleases Him.*
>
> ### The Message Version:
> *So Jesus tried again. "When you raise up the
> Son of Man, then you will know who I am—
> that I'm not making this up, but speaking only
> what the Father taught me. The One who sent
> me stays with me. He doesn't abandon me. He
> sees how much joy I take in pleasing him."*

Jesus consistently displayed initiative and therefore
fruitful signs and wonders followed His actions.
This was because Jesus *always* took pleasure in what
pleased God and in pleasing God. Jesus only

sought to demonstrate what God taught Him to say. We tend to delight in what pleases us, then try to attain fulfillment of our destiny and vision through our desires. Jesus delighted in what pleased God and then trusted God to fulfill His desires, destiny, and life's vision.

> **Psalms 37:4** - *Delight thyself also in the Lord; and he shall give thee the desires of thine heart.*

<u>*Delight* is *anag* in the Hebrew and means:</u>
1. to be soft or pliable, luxurious, effeminate
2. to sport, to be of dainty habit,
3. be pampered, to be happy about,
4. take exquisite delight, to make merry over

Delighting an act of surrendering to which we become sensitive and submissive to the things of God. His desires become the drive and declaration that cultivates and adorns our lives. Jesus said this was His initiative. He practiced such a lifestyle of delighting in God that He was able to state that even when you lift me on the cross, you will realize that what is being done (my life's vision), is only what pleases my Father.

Kingdom Initiative Decree

Father we repent for any way we have not taken initiative regarding our calling and destiny. We repent for every way we have been lazy, slothful, stagnant, and have only operated when we are seeking to be pleased or for our own temporary gain.

We repent for any way we have made our lives, callings, and visions be about us and not about you and truth regarding our purpose and destiny. We repent for any way we have not delighted in you and surrendered our lives to fully pleasing you and living to please you. We repent Jesus and fall out of agreement with selfishness, pride, entitlement, and idolatry of self.

We stop acting like we do not know what to do to fulfill destiny and the vision on our lives. We stop acting like we do not know what pleases you. We fall out of agreement with these lies and align with *John 8:32*. We know the truth and the truth is setting us free right now.

We SHIFT right now to living a lifestyle of doing what you have taught us, doing what you have and will tell us, and demonstrating our private conversations in our public lives.

We thank you Father for forgiving us and SHIFTING us to operating in consistent kingdom initiative.

Write The Vision

The bible itself is a compilation of God's purposes and plans for our lives, while providing further instructions for attaining what has been plainly written for us.

> *Revelation 1:10-11* - *I was in the Spirit [rapt in His power] on the Lord's Day, and I heard behind me a great voice like the calling of a war trumpet, saying, I am the Alpha and the Omega, the First and the Last. Write promptly what you see (your vision) in a book and send it to the seven churches which are in Asia--to Ephesus and to Smyrna and to Pergamum and to Thyatira and to Sardis and to Philadelphia and to Laodicea.*

> *Psalms 45:1* - *My heart is overflowing with a good matter: I speak of the things which I have made concerning the king: my tongue is the pen of a ready scribe.*

Even as God demonstrated the importance of writing the vision and making it plain, He encouraged us to follow in His footsteps.

> *Habakkuk 2:2-3* - *And the Lord answered me, and said, write the vision, and make it plain upon tables, that he may run that readeth it. For the vision is yet for an appointed time, but at the end it shall speak, and not lie: though it tarry, wait for it; because it will surely come, it will not tarry.*

Write in the Hebrew is *kathab* and means:
1. To write, record, enroll
2. To inscribe, engrave, write in, write on
3. To write down, describe in writing
4. To register, to decree
5. To be written, to be written down, be recorded, be enrolled

God does not need us to write the vision down so that He can bring it forth, as His word is going to accomplish His pleasures regardless of our actions. When a vision is written down, it serves as a literal tattoo of what God has spoken. What is written becomes an established seed or decree within the earth regarding what has been stated. Essentially it becomes an engraved prophecy that will reveal the will of God once it unfolds.

> *Isaiah 55:9-11 - For as the rain cometh down, and the snow from heaven, and returneth not thither, but watereth the earth, and maketh it bring forth and bud, that it may give seed to the sower, and bread to the eater: So shall my word be that goeth forth out of my mouth: it shall not return unto me void, but it shall accomplish that which I please, and it shall prosper in the thing whereto I sent it.*

God needs us to write the vision so that it can be fulfilled testimony that we ourselves and others, can plainly see and acknowledge. The written vision is prophecy of what has already been spoken and what is to come. The vision being written glorifies and testifies that God is a God of His word

37

and that He has already orchestrated plans for us, even before they were given to us to accomplish.

We definitely reap the benefits of achieving God's destiny and vision for our lives, but everything in life and about our lives was created to give God glory and to empower and establish Him in the earth. If it does not testify or glorify God, then we should not be doing it. Reading this sounds very selfish of God. *What reasons would God make everything be about Him?*

God is pure in every sense of His existence. When our focus is on fulfilling His ordained plan for life and our lives, we can all be who we are supposed to be and do what we are supposed to do, without projecting evil and harm upon one another. God is the foundation of our existence and when we remain rooted in our foundation, we can live in a world of harmony and love, where there is no darkness, godlessness (form) and void. By embracing, honoring and living for Him, we have constant fulfillment, positive growth and reproduction.

> **Genesis 1:1-4** - *In the beginning God created the heaven and the earth. And the earth was without form, and void; and darkness was upon the face of the deep. And the Spirit of God moved upon the face of the waters. And God said, Let there be light: and there was light. And God saw the light, that it was good: and God divided the light from the darkness.*

Light is *or* in the Hebrew and means:
1. Illumination, happiness, clear

2. Daybreak, morning, dawn, lightning
3. Light of lamp, light of life, light of prosperity
4. light of instruction, lift of face, Jehovah as Israel's light

When light goes forth, a revealing occurs. We can hear what God is saying for our lives, but when it is written – when we can see it and read it – a greater revealing manifests. We can see the good and prosperity in it. It becomes clear that these are not just words, but instructions and directions – a pattern given for our lives. The vision then SHIFTS from that which we are striving to bring forth, to being that which has already been brought forth, we are just producing what has already been fulfilled. This is important because we are always in a constant pursuit for something we think we need to attain. Yet our pursuit should be for more of God and what is of God, and then allowing Him to make plain what has already been destined for us.

Engraving The Vision Decree

God we take the time right now to write the vision, promises, and revelations that you have spoken to us, so that it will be plain to us, and testify to those who will see your vision come to pass in us. We contend even now that we have SHIFTED to being consistent writers of our visions and to governing our visions properly. We declare we will engrave them in the earth and bring them to pass with our lifestyle of embracing, honoring and living in the foundation and truth that you are our God and creator of everything. We fall out of agreement with pursuing creation, created things, and what we think will fulfill us. It is you God that makes the vision plain. You make it plain to us. You make it plain to others. And you make it plain in fulfilling it in the earth. We stop trying to do your job and stop trying to get you to do our job. We come into agreement with seeking you and allowing you to unfold your vision in us. Thank you God for being the author, revealer and visionary of our destiny and life's vision.

Assumptions That Thwart The Visions

It is important to note that our destiny and life's vision does not belong to a church, denomination, or a person. Our destiny and vision belongs to God, is for the building up of His body (His believers) such that we are equipped to go into the world and save (heal, deliver, set free) and establish His will and presence in the earth.

> *John 3:16 -* *For God so loved the world, that he gave his only begotten Son, that whosoever believeth in him should not perish, but have everlasting life.*

> *Ephesians 4:8-13 - Wherefore he saith, When he ascended up on high, he led captivity captive, and gave gifts unto men. (Now that he ascended, what is it but that he also descended first into the lower parts of the earth? He that descended is the same also that ascended up far above all heavens, that he might fill all things). And he gave some, apostles; and some, prophets; and some, evangelists; and some, pastors and teachers; for the perfecting of the saints, for the work of the ministry, for the edifying of the body of Christ: Till we all come in the unity of the faith, and of the knowledge of the Son of God, unto a perfect man, unto the measure of the stature of the fulness of Christ:*

The following is a list of assumptions and actions we tend to make when God reveals a vision to us:

41

- We assume that the people in our personal lives who are equipped to complete tasks in the vision have been called to help carry our vision
- We assume that because we attend a church/ministry, the vision should be submitted to that church/ministry
- We assume that because we attend a church/ministry, the leader/leaders should be the covering for our vision. They should have a revelation of our vision, be enthusiastic about the vision upon our lives, and assist us with bringing it to pass
- We assume that if we began a vision in a church/ministry, it should remain in that ministry. That ministry now owns the vision
- We assume that if one person covered the vision we cannot SHIFT if God is leading us. We assume it is disloyal to leave from under that covering
- We assume that every Godly vision is for the church and have to be done inside the church
- We assume that those who operate in a vision outside of a church or without leadership approval is rebellious *(No one accept family, believed the world flood but Noah kept building the ark – Genesis 5:32-10:1)*
- We assume that we have to do everything for the vision. We thus become overwhelmed and do not do anything. We can become prideful, fearful or lazy, while refusing to ask for help *(1Corinthians 3:6, Ephesians 4:8-11)*

- We assume that because people are not the same denomination as we are, they are not equipped to assist us in the vision (*Luke 9:14*)
- We assume that because people are not the same race, socioeconomic status, gender, lifestyle background, etc., as we are, they are not qualified to assist us with the vision
- We assume that everyone that assists us should have a position or title within the vision
- We assume that only the people we like, agree with us, and we think are anointed and ready for ministry should help us with our vision
- We assume that people have to be a certain age or saved for a certain period of time before they can help us with the vision
- We assume we have to be perfect and people have to be perfect to assist with the vision

Though these assumptions bear some truth, they are not always the case. Making such assumptions without seeking God's direction and counsel, can cause the vision to be hindered, thwarted and even aborted. When we connect or release the vision to the hands of people and systems that God has not said, we do God's job. We implement our own initiative instead of seeking God for His purpose and pleasures regarding who is to assist and how to go about fulfilling the vision. Religious and traditional strongholds, false loyalties, misperceptions, and errors to which scriptures have been taught and religiously indoctrinated, causes us to yield to assumptions that appear to be of God but either are not of Him or not His will for our destiny and vision. Assumptions regarding our visions and destinies can also cause unnecessary hurt. I say this because assumptions cause us to have expectations of people and systems that they were not meant to fulfill or carry. We are wanting people and systems to be things to us, do things for us, and assist us in ways God is not saying.

In *1Samuel 15*, we have Saul operating in his destiny as king of the Israelites. God gives Saul a vision to go smite the city of Amalek, to spare nothing - to utterly destroy all everything in the city.

> ***1Samuel 15:3*** - *Now go and smite Amalek, and utterly destroy all that they have, and spare them not; but slay both man and woman, infant and suckling, ox and sheep, camel and ass.*

King Saul gathered his people and they went to the city of Amalek and smote the Amalekites. King Saul however, spared the life of Agag, king of the Amalekites and kept the best of everything that was in the city of Amalek.

> ***Verse 9*** - *But Saul and the people spared Agag, and the best of the sheep, and of the oxen, and of the fatlings, and the lambs, and all that was good, and would not utterly destroy them: but every thing that was vile and refuse, that they destroyed utterly.*

God was so upset with Saul that he stated to Samuel that it repented Him to have made Saul king.

Verse 10-11 - *Then came the word of the Lord unto Samuel, saying, It repenteth me that I have set up Saul to be king: for he is turned back from following me, and hath not performed my commandments. And it grieved Samuel; and he cried unto the Lord all night.*

When Samuel confronted King Saul, he first acted as if he had accurately followed the plan of the Lord. But after being held accountable, he blamed sparing Agag and the best of the spoil, on the Israelites. He contended it was their idea.

Verse 15 - *And Saul said, they have brought them from the Amalekites: for the people spared the best of the sheep and of the oxen, to sacrifice unto the Lord thy God; and the rest we have utterly destroyed.*

Though Saul and the people took the spoil out of greed, the reasoning he gave Samuel was that they were going to offer these things up as a sacrifice unto the Lord.

Verse 18-21 - *And the Lord sent thee on a journey, and said, Go and utterly destroy the sinners the Amalekites, and fight against them until they be consumed. Wherefore then didst thou not obey the voice of the Lord, but didst fly upon the spoil, and didst evil in the sight of the Lord? And Saul said unto Samuel, Yea, I have obeyed the voice of the Lord, and have gone the way which the Lord sent me, and have brought Agag the king of Amalek, and have utterly destroyed the Amalekites. But the people took of the spoil, sheep and oxen, the chief of the things*

45

which should have been utterly destroyed, to
sacrifice unto the Lord thy God in Gilgal.

The challenge here is Saul was the vision carrier; so despite the desires of the people, he was responsible for making sure God's word came to pass. King Saul and the people allowed greed to open the door to a false assumption. Offering sacrifices unto God was deemed a great honor. Yet God had given specific directions and though offering sacrifices was good, it was not God's desire or design for this vision.

Because King Saul did not properly follow God's plan for the vision, made assumptions based on tradition and what pleased the people, God rejected him as king.

> **Verse 22-23** - *And Samuel said, hath the Lord as great delight in burnt offerings and sacrifices, as in obeying the voice of the Lord? Behold, to obey is better than sacrifice, and to hearken than the fat of rams. For rebellion is as the sin of witchcraft, and stubbornness is as iniquity and idolatry. Because thou hast rejected the word of the Lord, he hath also rejected thee from being king.*

God not only rejected King Saul, He stripped Saul of the destiny and vision as reigning king upon his life.

> **Verse 27-28** - *And as Samuel turned about to go away, he laid hold upon the skirt of his mantle, and it rent. And Samuel said unto him, The Lord hath rent the kingdom of Israel from thee this day,*

and hath given it to a neighbour of thine, that is
better than thou.

- I know you love your church
- I know you love your leaders and how much
  you want to be honoring to them and others
  who have been a part of your life
- I know you love the people around you and
  want their accolades, and want them to like
  you and speak highly of you
- I know you love things that feel good and
  look good
- I know you love traditions and religious
  rituals, and things that do and appear to
  please and honor God
- I know you want to partake in the glory that
  comes from the victory of the vision

I know because I have been there and have so
wanted these things and more. But I encourage you
to make sure your loyalty and allegiance is totally
to God. Anytime we exalt assumptions above the
word of God we fall into the sin of rebellion and
witchcraft as we become idolatrous in putting our
assumptions above God. We think we are
sacrificing and offering something up to God, but
what we are really sacrificing and crucifying is
God's word and plans.

The word *obey* in the Hebrew is *sama* and means:
1. To hear intelligently (often with implication of
   attention, obedience, etc.; causatively, to tell,
   etc.)

2. Attentively, call (gather) together, carefully, certainly, consent, consider, be content, declare, diligently, discern, give ear, discern
3. To hear (perceive by ear) to hear of or concerning
4. To hear (have power to hear) to hear with attention or interest, listen to
5. To understand (language), to hear (of judicial cases), to listen, give heed
6. To consent, agree to, grant request to, listen to, yield to, to obey, be obedient

Basically obey means to hear God clearly and do what He says. Many will not agree with it. Many will not understand it. Many will want you to sacrifice it. But they will not be the ones who will be rejected and stripped of the calling and destiny upon their lives. If you are not sure, do not assume anything and do not inject another plan. Continue to cultivate what you know God is saying, while waiting for Him to give you further direction for the destiny and vision for your life.

YOU ARE A CONTINUAL DIVINELY ORCHESTRATED PLAN THAT IS ALWAYS UNFOLDING!

Divine Connections

Just like King Saul had with Samuel, God will connect you to someone who will confirm, speak into, intercede, and hold you accountable to the destiny and vision for your life. This will not be a connection that you have to force upon someone or make happen. God will give this person or people a revelation of who you are and they will want to be who they should be in your life. They will want to see the destiny and vision upon your life come to pass.

> *Amos 3:3 - Can two walk together, except they be agreed?*

> *The Message Version - Do two people walk hand in hand if they aren't going to the same place?*

The word walk is *yalak* in the Greek and means:
1. to flow, to carry, to march,
2. to go, walk, come, depart, proceed, move, go away
3. prosper, pursue, cause to run, spread, take away ((- journey))

If you are having to force someone to understand the destiny and vision God has given you, then that is a good indication that this is not their role in your life.

If you are striving to prove to someone what God has spoken about you or striving to get someone to invest in what God has spoken about you, this is a good indication that this is not the role that person is to have in your life.

If someone or people are to be a part of the vision and calling on your life, there should be an agreement and a flow in your interactions. You will not have to play tug a war to get them to be who God has orchestrated them to be.

There are seasons and times for everything (*Ecclesiastes 3*). You hinder the flow to the vision by trying to interject people when it is not the proper time and season or it is simply not who they are to you.

- Some people may not be ready to walk with you
- Some people may not be meant to walk with you
- Some people may not know they are to walk with you
- Some people may have missed their season to walk with you

You have to move and operate in the momentum and God. And you have to respect the freewill of others even when they may be rejecting what you feel is God's will and plan. Regardless to what people do or do not do, if you are obedient to your destiny and vision, God will bless and honor you and your life's vision.

Psalms 75:7 - *But God is the judge: he putteth down one, and setteth up another.*

When you have to step out and do what God is desiring regarding your destiny and vision, do not chase gossip, seek to defend your actions, or retaliate against those who speak or work against you. The enemy is using these people and situations to distract and steal your focus, draw you into a fight that is not yours, and seeking to prove that you are not ready or fit for the destiny and vision you just stepped into.

You may have to constantly repent and release all anger, unforgiveness, hurt, anguish, frustration, rejection, fear, abandonment, and need or righteous justification to retaliate, while surrendering the battle to the Lord. Do this as much as you need to as it cleanses you from offense and attacks of the enemy. Do it every day, every hour, whatever it takes to keep you integral and honorable before the Lord. There will indeed come a day where you will react in laughter rather than offense. Keep doing it until that day unfolds. Know that God is going to honor your desire to do and be better than what was done to you, and honor your desire to assert and display His character and nature despite what has and will be done to you.

There are times when we have to step out into our destiny and life's visions that we are plagued by false loyalties, false delusions and misperceptions, and unhealthy alliances. We feel guilty for doing the will of God because we have been taught to honor our leaders and forsake not the assembly.

51

We are further informed that any defiance in this fashion is rebellion. Some of us have been cursed and told we would fail for being obedient to God. These words plague us and make us constantly question whether we made the right decision or heard God correctly. **Please be advised that there is nowhere in the bible where someone followed the plan of God and failed.** Saul's heart was not pure for the will and purposes of God that is the reason He was rejected and stripped of being king. If your heart is pure for God, He will restore you and put you on the right track if you did not hear correctly from Him.

> *Matthew 11:30 - Jesus said in the original Greek translation, Take My yoke upon you and learn of Me, for My yoke is easy and My burden is light and delightful.*

> **The Amplified Version** - *For My yoke is wholesome (useful, [a]good — not harsh, hard, sharp, or pressing, but comfortable, gracious, and pleasant), and My burden is light and easy to be borne.*

A *yoke* is a burden or bondage that places a person in slavery. Jesus says, *"His yoke is easy and His burden is light, delightful and easy to carry."* If Jesus' does not bind us, then no other yoke should place us in captivity. We should never feel burdened or in bondage when we are doing the work of the Lord. If we do feel yoked, we are carrying a false burden or we are allowing ourselves to be bound and controlled by religion, delusion, false loyalty or misplaced honor, or the wiles of the enemy. This is important because often we will remain in abusive religious relationships and situations due to yoking. We do not want to admit that we are experiencing abuse. We recognize the call and potential on our leaders' life and on the ministry, yet give way to confusion and witchcraft of mind binding and mind blinding because we do not want to admit that their fruit does not align with God. Moreover, we will justify the actions of our leaders because of their position and because of the cultural and religious scriptural yokes that have been passed down to us as honor. As an African American, I can contend that many in our culture are quick to bestow honor due to cultural and lifestyle similarities, hierarchy roles (well that is grandma, momma, pastor so we have to respect them regardless to what they do or say). We bestow entitlements and justifications as it relates to past experiences or bondages of slavery as we contend we deserve to act like a certain way or receive a not so justified reward because of what we or our ancestors have been through. This is a slave mentality that truly goes all the way back to when the Israelites were in Egypt. They felt entitled to have it easy in the wilderness due to being slaves of Pharaoh. This caused them to walk in doubt and idolatry as they were constantly questioning the provision and will of God. They were never able to SHIFT from a bondage mentality into realizing that God was meeting their every need as even in the wilderness, they had provision and manna that was likened unto the promised milk and honey.

> *Exodus 16:35* - *And the children of Israel did eat manna forty years, until they came to a land*

inhabited; they did eat manna, until they came unto the borders of the land of Canaan.

Deuteronomy 8:3-4 - *And He humbled you and allowed you to hunger and fed you with manna, which you did not know nor did your fathers know, that He might make you recognize and personally know that man does not live by bread only, but man lives by every word that proceeds out of the mouth of the Lord. Your clothing did not become old upon you nor did your feet swell these forty years.*

If we are truly honoring someone, it should not be at the expense of our own freedom in God. If anything, our honor of another person should further free us, while glorifying who that person is in God. Though we are to respect and honor our leadership, they should not abuse their position by lording over us. They should be submitted to God as we submit to them, and the fruit they display should be evidence that they are hearing and living for God, and have our best interest at heart.

Matthew 7:15-20 - *Beware of false prophets, which come to you in sheep's clothing, but inwardly they are ravening wolves. Ye shall know them by their fruits. Do men gather grapes of thorns, or figs of thistles? Even so every good tree bringeth forth good fruit; but a corrupt tree bringeth forth evil fruit. A good tree cannot bring forth evil fruit, neither can a corrupt tree bring forth good fruit. Every tree that bringeth not forth good fruit is hewn down, and cast into the fire. Wherefore by their fruits ye shall know them.*

54

Though all leaders and overseers do not hold the title of *bishop*, I would contend that *1Timothy 3:1-7* provides an adequate revelation of the fruit any leader or overseer should display.

The Amplified Version

The saying is true and irrefutable: If any man [eagerly] seeks the office of bishop (superintendent, overseer), he desires an excellent task (work). Now a bishop (superintendent, overseer) must give no grounds for accusation but must be above reproach, the husband of one wife, circumspect and temperate and self-controlled; [he must be] sensible and well behaved and dignified and lead an orderly (disciplined) life; [he must be] hospitable [showing love for and being a friend to the believers, especially strangers or foreigners, and be] a capable and qualified teacher,

Not given to wine, not combative but gentle and considerate, not quarrelsome but forbearing and peaceable, and not a lover of money [insatiable for wealth and ready to obtain it by questionable means].
He must rule his own household well, keeping his children under control, with true dignity, commanding their respect in every way and keeping them respectful.

For if a man does not know how to rule his own household, how is he to take care of the church of God? He must not be a new convert, or he may [develop a beclouded and stupid state of mind] as the result of pride [be blinded by conceit, and] fall

*into the condemnation that the devil [once] did.
Furthermore, he must have a good reputation and
be well thought of by those outside [the church],
lest he become involved in slander and incur
reproach and fall into the devil's trap.*

It is essential that we discern and be honest about
the fruit that is evident in peoples' lives, especially
our leaders.

> *1Thessalonians Chapter 5:12-14 - And we
> beseech you, brethren, to know them which labour
> among you, and are over you in the Lord, and
> admonish you; And to esteem them very highly in
> love for their work's sake. [And] be at peace
> among yourselves. Now we exhort you, brethren,
> warn them that are unruly, comfort the
> feebleminded, support the weak, be patient toward
> all [men].*

> *Hebrews 13:17 - Obey them that have the rule
> over you, and submit yourselves: for they watch
> for your souls, as they that must give account,
> that they may do it with joy, and not with grief:
> for that [is] unprofitable for you.*

How do we really esteem our leaders if we
empower them in a false representation of God's
character and nature? How do we esteem them and
justify our obedience and submission to them, if we
let them believe that it is okay to bind us and hold
us hostage to their false scriptural teachings and
demonic rule over our lives?

It is no way for our leaders to adequately admonish,
warn or keep watch over our souls, if they do not

have any revelation of the unhealthy fruit they may be displaying in their own lives. Even as we are held accountable to submitting, we are equally and more importantly held accountable to what we submit to.

> *1Corinthians 11:1 – Be yea followers of me, even as I also am of Christ*

> *1Corinthians 9:13-14 – Do ye not know that they which minister about holy things live of the things of the temple? And they which wait at the altar are partakers with the altar? Even so hath the Lord ordained that they which preach the gospel should live of the gospel.*

> *The Amplified Version -Do you not know that those men who are employed in the services of the temple get their food from the temple? And that those who tend the altar share with the altar [in the offerings brought]? [On the same principle] the Lord directed that those who publish the good news (the Gospel) should live (get their maintenance) by the Gospel.*

> *1Peter 5:2-3 - Feed the flock of God which is among you, taking the oversight thereof, not by constraint (force, binding), but willingly; not for filthy lucre (meanly, selfishly, self-seeking or eagerness for base gain), but of a ready mind; Neither as being lords over God's heritage, but being examples to the flock.*

Anybody want to shout right there?
Whewwwwwwww!!!!

Though there are instances, where God may lead you to confront a leader, sometimes it is best to assert your authority to be free and leave rather than contend with a leader who has no intention of changing. Unless you have an assignment to complete or God is leading you to stay to teach you some things, it is best to seek Him for a ministry that can empower you and the vision in you. In transitioning it is importance to admit and accept that you are being abused and mistreated. Admittance and acceptance empowers us in the truth that what we are experiencing is not God's will, and we have a choice to get out of bondage. Be respectful in letting the leader know you are leaving. They may not give you their blessing, but it is more important to be in God's will and to demonstrate his nature and do as he desires than to remain in bondage.

Another challenge with connecting ourselves to people rather than allowing God to connect us, is that we risk leaders pimping us by using our gifting. Yet they are not invested in releasing us in the calling and vision on our lives. Pimping is exploitation of someone's purity and limitations for personal gain. We are good enough to be used to do exploits to advance their vision, but we are not good enough to be empowered and released in our exploits to advance God's vision on our lives.

> *Colossians 2:8* - *Beware lest any man spoil you through philosophy and vain deceit, after the tradition of men, after the rudiments of the world, and not after Christ.*

The Amplified Version - See to it that no one carries you off as spoil or makes you yourselves captive by his so- called philosophy and intellectualism and vain deceit (idle fancies and plain nonsense), following human tradition (men's ideas of the material rather than the spiritual world), just crude notions following the rudimentary and elemental teachings of the universe and disregarding [the teachings of] Christ (the Messiah).

Spoil in Greek is *sylagogeo* and means:
1. To lead away as booty, i. e. (figuratively) seduce, spoil
2. To carry off booty, to carry one off as a captive (and slave),
3. To lead away from the truth and subject to one's sway

"Lead away as booty?" Really??? Anyone else challenged at the thought of being pimped?

1Peter 2:3 - And through covetousness shall they with feigned words make merchandise of you: whose judgment now of a long time lingereth not, and their damnation slumbereth not.

The Message Version - They're only out for themselves. They'll say anything, anything, that sounds good to exploit you. They won't, of course, get by with it. They'll come to a bad end, for God has never just stood by and let that kind of thing go on.

Romans 16:18 - For such people are not serving our Lord Christ, but their own appetites. By smooth talk and flattery they deceive the minds of naive people.

2Corinthians 2:17 - *Unlike so many, we do not peddle the word of God for profit. On the contrary, in Christ we speak before God with sincerity, as those sent from God.*

2Peter 1:16 - *For we did not follow cleverly devised stories when we told you about the coming of our Lord Jesus Christ in power, but we were eyewitnesses of his majesty.*

Jude 1:16 - *These people are grumblers and faultfinders; they follow their own evil desires; they boast about themselves and flatter others for their own advantage.*

SHIFT and let God connect you to the leaders and relationships that He has ordained for your destiny and life's vision.

Once you SHIFT into the divine connections and operate in the vision that God has called you to, it is important to do better than what was being done to you. It will be important to allow God to heal you of any hurts that came from old relationships, realizations of being pimped, abused, unsupported, recognized or validated in who you are and what God is saying about you. God will even require you to express love and even minister to those that hurt you. This will be a difficult season to work through as you will want to retaliate due to feeling justified in your belief and actions. One thing I am learning as a visionary is that God is about reconciliation (unity and restoring harmony) and even restoration (mending relationships and walking in some form of fellowship again). In prayer one day God spoke this revelation to me and then gave me these passages of scriptures:

> *Justice at the expense of tearing someone down is revenge. Real justice is providing the opportunity to pull and build someone up even when they have torn you down. The pure love of justice is not gloating because that person now needs you, but joying that you got to demonstrate God's pure love in helping transform that person's life, SHIFTING them into my true love.*

> ### *Matthew 5:13-16 - The Message Version*
> *Let me tell you why you are here. You're here to be salt—seasoning that brings out the God-flavors of this earth. If you lose your saltiness, how will people taste godliness? You've lost your usefulness and will end up in the garbage. Here's another way to put it: You're here to be light, bringing out the God-colors in the world. God is not a secret to be kept. We're going public with this, as public as a city on a hill. If I make you light—bearers, you don't think I'm going to hide you under a bucket, do you? I'm putting you on a light stand. Now that I've put you there on a hilltop, on a light stand--shine! Keep open house; be generous with your lives. By opening up to others, you'll prompt people to open up with God, this generous Father in heaven.*

> ### *Matthew 5:44-48 - The Message Version*
> *I'm challenging that. I'm telling you to love your enemies. Let them bring out the best in you, not the worst. When someone gives you a hard time,*

respond with the energies of prayer, for then you are working out of your true selves, your God–created selves. This is what God does. He gives his best––the sun to warm and the rain to nourish––to everyone, regardless: the good and bad, the nice and nasty. If all you do is love the lovable, do you expect a bonus? Anybody can do that. You simply say hello to those who greet you, do you expect a medal? Any run–of–the–mill sinner does that. In a word, what I'm saying is, grow up. You're kingdom subjects. Now live like it. Live out your God–created identity. Live generously and graciously toward others, the way God lives toward you.

I have had to learn how to really forgive those who hurt me and be open to reconciling and restoring relationships as God leads. In these instances it will be your relationship with God and your drive to please Him that will give you the fortitude to obey Him and demonstrate His character. Ultimately our destinies and visions are not worth remaining in bitterness and unforgiveness. We must strive to live a life of displaying the true essence of God even at the expense of blessing our enemies.

Divine Connections Decree

Lord I release every person who is not supposed to be a part of my destiny and vision. I repent for striving to make them be more to me than you have design and ask for forgiveness of any unnecessary hurt and anguish I have caused them and myself.

Lord I fall out of agreement with all false loyalty, false honor and delusion, misrepresentation, spirit of control and abuse, and false allegiance. I admit and accept that I have been mistreated and abused, forgive the abuser, and decree a cleansing and healing through the blood of Jesus, of all abusive seeds, manifestations, and hurts in the name of Jesus. I break every demonic soul tie with the abuser and those who have hurt me, and with the ministry that misused and mishandled me. In the name of Jesus I fall out of agreement with every binding, blinding, demonic yoking, spirit of control and manipulation, bewitchment, intimidation tactic, and seduction tied to those leaders and that ministry. I break every allegiance and alliance to the abuser and user and to the ministry, as it relates to my giftings, calling, destiny, the vision for my life, my finances, and generational heritage. I declare that I am no longer bound by any curse, demonic assignment or legal right of the enemy that is connected to the abuser or that ministry and repent for anyway I was not admittedly truthful or discerning of the unhealthy fruit and bondage the abuser and this ministry operated in.

Lord I forgive every person who has spoken and worked against your destiny and vision for my life.

I repent for being unforgiving, angry, hurt, rejected, frustrated, and for wanting to give them a piece of my mind or bring harm to them. I repent and ask you to cleanse me of all offense and rage and ask that you cleanse them of any offense and fiery darts my thoughts and words may have sent against them.

I decree I will be one that will do better than was done to me. I decree I will not backbite, throw stones, retaliate, and will only share the truth and release judgment as you lead me. If you are not leading me, I will shut up and shut down any conversation or behavior that will attempt to draw me into sinning through gossip and retaliation.

I thank you God even now that your signs and wonders will speak for me. I thank you even now that the success of my destiny and vision will reveal the importance of my obedience and allegiance to you. I even thank you for the opportunity to minister with and minister to those who have rejected and hurt me. You are a God of reconciliation and restoration. I surrender every righteous justification so that you can get glory out of my life and align and draw your people back to you. Thank you for being God and for orchestrating every portion of my existence. I certainly appreciate all that you are and do.

Lord I ask that the eyes of my understanding be enlightened so that I may precisely discern and connect to those you have ordained to be a part of my destiny and vision. I repent for any way I have rejected my divine connections, operated in a respect of persons' mentality, and have not followed through with what you have told me to do in order that I may divinely connect with them. I align and receive my divine connections into my life right now in the name of Jesus. I thank you for the agreement and flow we operate in even now. I thank you for the divine connections that would even mentor and provide me godly counsel as I build the vision even now (*Psalms 1*). I thank you that they desire to walk with me and desire to see your will come to pass for my life even now. I thank you that my life is enhanced by them and they are enhanced by me and that you are getting glory out of our destinies and life's visions even now.

God Makes The Vision Plain

God chooses who is to carry the vision, and provides the necessity and purpose for the vision.

> *Proverbs 29:18 New English Translation* - *Where there is no prophetic vision the people cast off restraint, but blessed is he who keeps the law.*

> *The Amplified Version* - *Where there is no vision [no redemptive revelation of God], the people perish; but he who keeps the law [of God, which includes that of man]--blessed (happy, fortunate, and enviable) is he.*

When God chooses you to carry a vision, it is important to hear Him clearly concerning the vision.

> *Numbers 12:6* - *And He said, hear now My words: If there is a prophet among you, I the Lord make Myself known to him in a vision and speak to him in a dream.*

> *Ephesians 1:17* - *[For I always pray to] the God of our Lord Jesus Christ, the Father of glory, that He may grant you a spirit of wisdom and revelation [of insight into mysteries and secrets] in the [deep and intimate] knowledge of Him.*

> *Galatians 1:11:12* - *For I want you to know, brethren, that the Gospel which was proclaimed and made known by me is not man's gospel [a human invention, according to or patterned after any human standard]. For indeed I did not receive it from man, nor was I taught it, but [it*

*came to me] through a [direct] revelation [given]
by Jesus Christ (the Messiah).*

When God chooses you to release a vision, it is
important to seek God for the following:

- *Who the vision is for* (everyone, the
  unsaved, hurting women or men, children,
  politicians, business owners)
- *Where should the vision be* located (in a
  church, community, in a prison, in a school,
  Texas, Chicago)
- *Who is to cover the vision* (your present
  leadership, the church around the corner, a
  ministry in another state that has a similar
  vision, a mentor or spiritual parent, or
  should only Jesus cover the ministry)
- *Who is to assist with bringing the vision to
  pass* (a few people you already know,
  people you do not know that God will
  connect you with, the tongue talking
  Catholics around town, the youth at church,
  the students at the college in your
  neighborhood, an online ministry)

We see the importance of allowing God to reveal
every facet of our destiny and vision in the story of
Moses (*Study Exodus 2-14*). God called Moses to be
a deliverer. The vision was for Moses to deliver the
Israelites into the promise land. Though Moses
operated in adequacy which challenged his ability
to effectively achieve his calling and life's vision,
God provided everything Moses needed to fulfill
the calling and vision on his life.

God provided Moses with the following:

- **The destiny and vision for his life**
  Exodus 3:10 - *Come now therefore, and I will send thee unto Pharaoh, that thou mayest bring forth my people the children of Israel out of Egypt.*

- **The purpose for the vision and who was to be delivered**
  Exodus 3:7-8 - *And the Lord said, I have surely seen the affliction of my people which are in Egypt, and have heard their cry by reason of their taskmasters; for I know their sorrows; And I am come down to deliver them out of the hand of the Egyptians, and to bring them up out of that land unto a good land and a large, unto a land flowing with milk and honey; unto the place of the Canaanites, and the Hittites, and the Amorites, and the Perizzites, and the Hivites, and the Jebusites.*

- **Where the vision was to take place**
  Exodus 4:19 - *And the Lord said unto Moses in Midian, Go, return into Egypt: for all the men are dead which sought thy life. And Moses took his wife and his sons, and set them upon an ass, and he returned to the land of Egypt: and Moses took the rod of God in his hand.*

- **Revelation that God sent Moses to complete the vision**
  Exodus 3:13-14 - *And Moses said unto God, Behold, when I come unto the children of Israel, and shall say unto them, The God of your fathers hath sent me unto you; and they shall say to me,*

What is his name? what shall I say unto them?
And God said unto Moses, I Am That I Am: and
he said, Thus shalt thou say unto the children of
Israel, I Am hath sent me unto you.

- **Witnesses who need the vision, will**
  confirm the vision, and will come into
  alignment with the vision
  Exodus 3:16: 18 - Go, and gather the elders of
  Israel together, and say unto them, The Lord God
  of your fathers, the God of Abraham, of Isaac, and
  of Jacob, appeared unto me, saying, I have surely
  visited you, and seen that which is done to you in
  Egypt: And I have said, I will bring you up out
  of the affliction of Egypt unto the land of the
  Canaanites, and the Hittites, and the Amorites,
  and the Perizzites, and the Hivites, and the
  Jebusites, unto a land flowing with milk and
  honey. And they shall hearken to thy voice: and
  thou shalt come, thou and the elders of Israel,
  unto the king of Egypt, and ye shall say unto
  him, The Lord God of the Hebrews hath met with
  us: and now let us go, we beseech thee, three
  days' journey into the wilderness, that we may
  sacrifice to the Lord our God.

- **Revelation of the obstacles to the vision**
  Exodus 3:19 - And I am sure that the king of
  Egypt will not let you go, no, not by a mighty
  hand.

- **How to handle the obstacles to the vision**
  Exodus 3:20 - And I will stretch out my hand,
  and smite Egypt with all my wonders which I
  will do in the midst thereof: and after that he will
  let you go.

69

- **The weapons to fulfill the vision**
  *Exodus 4:2-4 - And the Lord said unto him,
  What is that in thine hand? And he said, A rod.
  And he said, Cast it on the ground. And he cast it
  on the ground, and it became a serpent; and
  Moses fled from before it. And the Lord said unto
  Moses, Put forth thine hand, and take it by the
  tail. And he put forth his hand, and caught it, and
  it became a rod in his hand:*

- **Confidence, trainings, giftings, divine
  assistances and connections with bringing
  the vision to pass**
  *Exodus 4:10-17 - And Moses said unto the Lord,
  O my Lord, I am not eloquent, neither heretofore,
  nor since thou hast spoken unto thy servant: but I
  am slow of speech, and of a slow tongue. And the
  Lord said unto him, Who hath made man's
  mouth? or who maketh the dumb, or deaf, or the
  seeing, or the blind? have not I the Lord? Now
  therefore go, and I will be with thy mouth, and
  teach thee what thou shalt say. And he said, O
  my Lord, send, I pray thee, by the hand of him
  whom thou wilt send. And the anger of the Lord
  was kindled against Moses, and he said, Is not
  Aaron the Levite thy brother? I know that he can
  speak well. And also, behold, he cometh forth to
  meet thee: and when he seeth thee, he will be glad
  in his heart. And thou shalt speak unto him, and
  put words in his mouth: and I will be with thy
  mouth, and with his mouth, and will teach you
  what ye shall do. And he shall be thy spokesman
  unto the people: and he shall be, even he shall be
  to thee instead of a mouth, and thou shalt be to*

him instead of God. And thou shalt take this rod in thine hand, wherewith thou shalt do signs.

Exodus 7:1-2 - And the Lord said unto Moses, See, I have made thee a god to Pharaoh: and Aaron thy brother shall be thy prophet. Thou shalt speak all that I command thee: and Aaron thy brother shall speak unto Pharaoh, that he send the children of Israel out of his land.

- **Favor and provision to progress the vision**
  Exodus 3:21-22 - And I will give this people favour in the sight of the Egyptians: and it shall come to pass, that, when ye go, ye shall not go empty. But every woman shall borrow of her neighbour, and of her that sojourneth in her house, jewels of silver, and jewels of gold, and raiment: and ye shall put them upon your sons, and upon your daughters; and ye shall spoil the Egyptians.

- **Strategies needed to fulfill the vision** (God gave countless strategies to Moses all throughout his journey as a deliverer to accomplish the destiny and vision on His life. *Study Exodus 1-17)*
  Exodus 7:1-5 - And the Lord said unto Moses, See, I have made thee a god to Pharaoh: and Aaron thy brother shall be thy prophet. Thou shalt speak all that I command thee: and Aaron thy brother shall speak unto Pharaoh, that he send the children of Israel out of his land. And I will harden Pharaoh's heart, and multiply my signs and my wonders in the land of Egypt. But Pharaoh shall not hearken unto you, that I may lay my hand upon Egypt, and bring forth mine

71

armies, and my people the children of Israel, out of the land of Egypt by great judgments. And the Egyptians shall know that I am the Lord, when I stretch forth mine hand upon Egypt, and bring out the children of Israel from among them.

- **The end destination to fulfilling the vision**
  Exodus 3:8 - And I am come down to deliver them out of the hand of the Egyptians, and to bring them up out of that land unto a good land and a large, unto a land flowing with milk and honey; unto the place of the Canaanites, and the Hittites, and the Amorites, and the Perizzites, and the Hivites, and the Jebusites.

Obedient Commitment To The Vision

In exploring the costs and effects of our destiny and life's vision, it is important to note that choice will cost you everything.

> *Luke 14:25-28* - *And there went great multitudes with him: and he turned, and said unto them, if any man come to me, and hate not his father, and mother, and wife, and children, and brethren, and sisters, yea, and his own life also, he cannot be my disciple. And whosoever doth not bear his cross, and come after me, cannot be my disciple. For which of you, intending to build a tower, sitteth not down first, and counteth the cost, whether he have sufficient to finish it?*

<u>Intend</u> in the Greek is *thelo* and means:
1. To determine (as an active option from subjective impulse
2. Choose or prefer (literally or figuratively); by implication, to wish, i. e. be inclined to (sometimes adverbially, gladly); impersonally for the future tense, to be about to; by Hebraism, to delight in:— desire, be disposed (forward), to will, have in mind, intend, to be resolved or determined
3. To purpose, to desire, to wish, to love to, like to do a thing
4. Be fond of doing, to take delight in, have pleasure

Even as we examine the cost and explore our intentions, we realize that obedience is a choice.

73

We have to choose to commit to the will of God and follow through with what He has orchestrated for our lives. Our obedience is a determinant for the success of our destiny and calling.

> **Verse 29-30 -** *Lest haply, after he hath laid the foundation, and is not able to finish it, all that behold it begin to mock him, saying, This man began to build, and was not able to finish.*

When choosing obedience you come into agreement with what God is requiring of you and you are able to handle obstacles and tower in whatever God is requiring to complete the vision.

> **Acts 9: 10-11 -** *Now there was in Damascus a disciple named Ananias. The Lord said to him in a vision, Ananias. And he answered, Here am I, Lord. And the Lord said to him, Get up and go to the street called Straight and ask at the house of Judas for a man of Tarsus named Saul, for behold, he is praying [there].*

> **1Thessalonians 5:20 -** *Do not spurn the gifts and utterances of the prophets [do not depreciate prophetic revelations nor despise inspired instruction or exhortation or warning].*

> **Ecclesiastes 5:4-5 The Message Version -** *When you tell God you'll do something, do it-- now. God takes no pleasure in foolish gabble. Vow it, then do it. Far better not to vow in the first place than to vow and not pay up.*

74

The Amplified Version - When you vow a vow or make a pledge to God, do not put off paying it; for God has no pleasure in fools (those who witlessly mock Him). Pay what you vow. It is better that you should not vow than that you should vow and not pay.

As you choose obedience, it is essential to come into covenant with what God is desiring by making a vow to successfully achieve your destiny and life's vision.

James 5:12 - But above all things, my brethren, swear not, neither by heaven, neither by the earth, neither by any other oath: but let your yea be yea; and [your] nay, nay; lest ye fall into condemnation.

Deuteronomy 23:21-23 - The Message Version - When you make a vow to God, your God, don't put off keeping it; God, your God, expects you to keep it and if you don't you're guilty. But if you don't make a vow in the first place, there's no sin. If you say you're going to do something, do it. Keep the vow you willingly vowed to God, your God. You promised it, so do it.

Dictionary.com defines *vow* as:
1. A solemn promise, pledge, or personal commitment: marriage vows; a vow of secrecy.
2. A solemn promise made to a deity or saint committing oneself to an act, service, or condition.
3. A solemn or earnest declaration.

Vowing to God allows us to take ownership in being obedient to the vision and makes us responsible to bringing it to past.

> *Isaiah 59:21* - *As for me, this [is] my covenant with them, saith the LORD; My spirit that [is] upon thee, and my words which I have put in thy mouth, shall not depart out of thy mouth, nor out of the mouth of thy seed, nor out of the mouth of thy seed's seed, saith the LORD, from henceforth and for ever.*

As we remain constant with keeping our vow with God, our spiritual appetite increases and is even fulfilled in the rewards that comes from being obedient.

> *John 4:34* - *Jesus said to them, My food is to do the will of him who sent me and to accomplish his work.*

> *The Amplified Version* - *Jesus said to them, My food (nourishment) is to do the will (pleasure) of Him Who sent Me and to accomplish and completely finish His work.*

Obedience Decree

Lord I thank you for choosing me as a vision carrier. I accept my destiny and call, and seek you clearly for what you are desiring concerning the vision. Even now I cleanse my senses to hear you with precision and I make a vow to do your will despite the cost.

I SHIFT to journeying on the street called *"Straight"* so that I can be properly aligned to hear everything you are speaking and operate as you are requiring me.

I thank you for your prophetic utterances and revelations, and respect and commit to following through with your instructions. I thank you for writing the vision and making it plain in my life, for exhorting me in the vision, and for revealing all warnings and provisions needed for the vision.

Obedience is my portion Lord as I understand that obedience is better than sacrifice *(1Samuel 15:22)*. I sacrifice myself and my own will for the sake of obedience, while rejecting all stubbornness, rebellion, witchcraft and idolatry that would hinder me from properly flowing in the vision *(1Samuel 15:23)*.

I receive your fruit of agreement, compliance and conformity and glory in releasing the vision for you and seeing you get glory out of my life. Thank you Lord for choosing me for the vision.

Leading & Administrating

Leading and administrating are two very different attributes. They both go hand in hand when journeying in your destiny and when initially building the foundation of a vision. If either one is missing it will hinder the structured foundation of the ministry.

Dictionary.com defines *lead* as:
1. To go before or with to show the way, conduct or escort
2. To conduct by holding and guiding
3. To influence or induce, cause
4. To guide in direction, course, action, opinion, etc., bring
5. To conduct or bring (water, wire, etc.) in a particular course

Dictionary.com defines *leader* as:
1. A person or thing that leads
2. A guiding or directing head, as of an army, movement, or political group

Dictionary.com defines *administrate* as:
1. To manage (affairs, a government, etc.), have executive charge of, to administer the law
2. To bring into use or operation
3. To make application of, give
4. To supervise the formal taking of (an oath or the like)
5. A person who manages or has a talent for managing

6. Work in an administrative capacity, supervise or be in charge of
7. handle, manage, care, deal, be in charge of, act on, or dispose of,
8. Oversee, superintend, supervise, manage, watch and direct

A leader is someone who is hands on. They role model by getting in and doing the work. Leaders instruct, teach, guide, empower, train, while leading and demonstrating what they are equipping others to do.

An administrator is someone who oversees and manages a work in and within the vision. An administrator can be hands on at times, but mostly an administrator offers suggestions and delegate duties. They offer suggestions and ideas, delegate the duties, and then manage the project to make sure things get done.

As the vision carrier and when choosing leaders to assist with the vision, the person/people will have to possess both attributes to effectively build the visions. The visionary and leaders will not only have to do the work, teach, guide, instruct, empower, but you all will also have to explore, implement and facilitate ideas, tasks, and strategies that are in line with the vision. When operating in both, the visionary, leaders, those that are partaking of the vision, and the visions itself, productively can grow on a solid foundation that can be sustained and maintained.

Before launching a vision and when choosing leaders, it is essential to know if you and the leaders have the ability to lead and administrate and which area each of you need to grow in and need assistance in.

As we explore this consideration, explore the following questions to discern where each of you are. It is important to be honest in your abilities so that you will know where you need to improve and where you need to acquire assistance as a vision carrier and in relations to efficient leaders to assist with the vision. Questions to consider:

1. Which area of the vision has called you to overseer? What reason has God chose you in this area? Be detailed in your response.
2. Is this is the season or time to be in this role? Explain your response
3. What is your perception of the attributes of leading and administrating?
4. Do you possess the ability to lead and administrate? How so? Be detailed.
5. Where do you need to grow as a leader and administrator? Are you committed to learning and growing as a leader and administrator? Pursue ways to grow in this area and become consistent so you can be efficient in these areas.
6. Which attribute do you need the assistance of others in and what type of assistance do you need?
7. Do you have the zeal to lead and administrate in the vision or area you are

overseeing? What healing or person improvement do you need to improve your zeal?

Leadership Scriptures

> **Romans 12:8 The Amplified Version** - *He who exhorts (encourages), to his exhortation; he who contributes, let him do it in simplicity and liberality; he who gives aid and superintends, with zeal and singleness of mind; he who does acts of mercy, with genuine cheerfulness and joyful eagerness.*

> **Matthew 20:25-28 the Amplified Version** - *And Jesus called them to Him and said, You know that the rulers of the Gentiles lord it over them, and their great men hold them in subjection [tyrannizing over them]. Not so shall it be among you; but whoever wishes to be great among you must be your servant, And whoever desires to be first among you must be your slave — Just as the Son of Man came not to be waited on but to serve, and to give His life as a ransom for many [the price paid to set them free].*

A Good Leader Possesses The Following Characteristics:

- Exude and constantly strive to operate in the nature and character of God
- Supreme motivator - able to esteem and encourage others in purity and without any hidden motives
- Effectively communicate, inspire, motivate and give clear/sound direction or at least motivate

and encourage others to invests in the vision even if the fullness of it has been revealed

- Pursues the eyes, ears and heart of Christ and for the vision; sees a person and the vision beyond where they are and for who they are, and esteem, teach, impart, activate, and help process them and the vision to that place
- Discerns and prays concerning the team members personal calling in Christ and provide avenues for them to operate in the calling
- Lead and follow
- Delegate duties based on callings and step back and allow the person/persons to operate in that assignment while giving grace for mistakes made and constructive criticism that helps them progress forward in healthiness
- Shift team members from a mindset of not just being utilized in giftings and talents but understanding and cultivating the calling and full destiny on the lives of team members
- Effectively communicate with all types of people and even to explore difficult issues, even if it is issues the team/member has with the leader or a decision a leader makes
- Be sensitive to the personal issues of team members and can decipher when deliverance and healing issues are necessary for assisting that person in progressing towards healthy maturity in the Lord
- Seeks to be spiritually and emotionally healthy by constantly striving to improve self and creates avenues to improve others
- Comfortable with making mistakes and admiring them while realigning self and the vision with correcting what has been wrong

- Repents quickly, solves personal issues in a healthy and timely manner and doesn't allow personal challenges to affect his or her communication with others or the ability to adequately lead the group
- Maintain balance between the vision and personal life; discerns when to rest and refresh ones' self, the team and the vision
- Fear God not man and allows God to be the source of his or her strength, success, and promotion
- Is humble, confident, and mature in the things of the Lord
- Has a sense of humor; can laugh at self, Satan, and in the face of adversity
- Be faithful to the services and visions of their covering, local assembly, and faithful in seeing the vision of God come to past within the group
- Does not mind praying and fasting and sacrificing time, self, and desires for the good of the vision
- Creative, inventive, and ambitious; passionate for the things and people of God
- Be honest, fair in judgment; pursues the eyes and will of the Lord so that His will can be established in people, situations, and environment
- Extends grace without holding grudges, or harboring resentment or unforgiveness
- Assertive, competent, confident, courageous, bold when necessary, and forthright
- Open to allowing God to be free to move without building high places on areas of success, yet trusting that God can do above and beyond one's last or previous success

- Flexible, open to change and operating in the timing and movement of the Lord
- Remain rooted and grounded in the word, pursues and operates in the truth of the Lord
- Pursues the fullness of the Holy Spirit and gifts of the spirit operating in his or her life or ministry

Administrative Scriptures

> ***1Corinthians 12: 27-28 The Amplified Version*** - *Now you [collectively] are Christ's body and [individually] you are members of it, each part severally and distinct [each with his own place and function].*
> *So God has appointed some in the church [for His own use]: first apostles (special messengers); second prophets (inspired preachers and expounders); third teachers; then wonder- workers; then those with ability to heal the sick; helpers; administrators; [speakers in] different (unknown) tongues.*
>
> ***1Corinthians 14:40 The Amplified Version*** - *But all things should be done with regard to decency and propriety and in an orderly fashion.*
>
> - *Jesus organized His ministry by choosing his inner circle of three disciples (Mark 9:2), appointing the twelve (Mark 3:13-14), and sending out the seventy two by two (Luke 10:1)*
> - *Joseph (Genesis 41:41-57; 47:13-26)*
> - *Jethro (Exodus 18), and Titus (Titus 1:5) all demonstrate the gift of administration.*

A Good Administrator Possesses The Following Characteristics:

- Excited about the vision and about fulfilling tasks and duties
- Can hear God for strategies and consistent witty ideas that improve and advance the ministry
- Able to use strategies and witty ideas to obtain favor, blessings, save money
- A people person or at least open to engage with all types of people
- Have great communication skills and can effectively communicate and give direction and guidance with clarity
- Wise and mature and live a balance and mature lifestyle
- Able to empower others to fulfill tasks and carry the vision
- A natural organizer - organized and able to organize people, projects, tasks, money, goals, departments within the vision
- Able to multitask and can successfully administrate several projects at one time
- Are able to solve problems and diffuse challenging conflicts and situations
- See the future of the vision and can implement ideas, strategies, tools, etc., to progress the vision forward
- Understands the importance of not just using people to complete tasks and fulfill roles, but are great motivators and personally esteem team members and workers
- Humble, respectful, honoring, and careful not to bully, belittle and control and manipulate people

- Willing to be hands on when necessary to complete tasks
- Can recognize when he or she is overwhelmed and need to rest and refresh
- Balanced in fasting, praying, studying the word, while accomplishing administrating duties
- Good decision maker and able to step in and run and assist with the vision and overseeing parts of the vision when necessary
- Operates in a spirit of excellence and is willing to make personal improvements and improvements to the vision and team such that it produces excellent results
- Possess professional skills of an administrator or business to effectively assist with events, meetings, vision tasks

Team Empowerment

When Jesus came upon his divine connections, he knew who they were and encouraged them to take their rightful place in His

ministry. Though a couple of them wanted to go finalize personal endeavors, they did not reject Jesus and eagerly accepted their calling to His ministry vision. This yields revelation that we should know who is to assist in the vision and they should confirm their position within the vision.

> *Matthew 4:18-22 - And Jesus, walking by the sea of Galilee, saw two brethren, Simon called Peter, and Andrew his brother, casting a net into the sea: for they were fishers. And he saith unto them, Follow me, and I will make you fishers of men. And they straightway left their nets, and followed him. And going on from thence, he saw other two brethren, James the son of Zebedee, and John his brother, in a ship with Zebedee their father, mending their nets; and he called them. And they immediately left the ship and their father, and followed him.*

God revealed who was to assist me in building the vision of my ministry. I then approached them for confirmation of what God was speaking. I asked them to pray and ask God if they are to be a part of the vision, their purpose and what God desired of them as a vision member and as it related to their destiny and calling on their lives. Every six months to a year, I meet with each vision member to examine their purpose for being a part of the vision and make adjustments as God leads. Their purpose may have changed, the season could be over or more commitment, growth or opportunity is needed regarding who they are to the vision and in the kingdom to God.

As a vision carrier, you determine the mood and enthusiasm of the vision, and how others respond or take ownership of the vision. When Jesus commissioned and sent out the 12 disciples, he provided a clear vision of what to expect and what their mandate was as disciples, while empowering them in their giftings, callings and life works.

> *Matthew 10:5-15*
> *These twelve Jesus sent forth, and commanded them, saying, Go not into the way of the Gentiles, and into any city of the Samaritans enter ye not: But go rather to the lost sheep of the house of Israel. And as ye go, preach, saying, the kingdom of heaven is at hand. Heal the sick, cleanse the lepers, raise the dead, cast out devils: freely ye have received, freely give.*
>
> *Provide neither gold, nor silver, nor brass in your purses, nor scrip for your journey, neither two coats, neither shoes, nor yet staves: for the workman is worthy of his meat. And into whatsoever city or town ye shall enter, enquire who in it is worthy; and there abide till ye go thence. And when ye come into an house, salute it. And if the house be worthy, let your peace come upon it: but if it be not worthy, let your peace return to you.*

And whosoever shall not receive you, nor hear your words, when ye depart out of that house or city, shake off the dust of your feet. Verily I say unto you, it shall be more tolerable for the land of Sodom and Gomorrah in the day of judgment, than for that city.

The disciples knew:
- what to expect from those partaking of the vision
- what was expected of them as vision members
- how to respond to rejecters and partakers of the vision
- the importance of manifesting signs and wonders
- they were supported by Jesus in producing greater works
- they were to advance the kingdom not just through the vision but through who they were in God
- that miracles signs and wonders was their portion

Jesus sent them out with the intent for them to operate in their calling and to produce the vision.

Matthew 9:35-38 - And Jesus went about all the cities and villages, teaching in their synagogues, and preaching the gospel of the kingdom, and healing every sickness and every disease among the people. But when he saw the multitudes, he was moved with compassion on them, because they fainted, and were scattered abroad, as sheep having no shepherd. Then saith he unto his disciples, The harvest truly is plenteous, but the labourers are few; Pray ye therefore the Lord of the harvest, that he will send forth labourers into his harvest.

Jesus imparted and equipped the disciples for the same opportunities He had to reach the masses and to do even greater works than He did.

John 14:12 - *Verily, verily, I say unto you, He that believes on me, the works that I do shall he do also; and greater works than these shall he do; because I go unto my Father.*

As vision carriers, we should be empowering those around us to be better and progress even farther than we do.

Philippians 2:3-4 New International Version *- Do nothing from selfishness or empty conceit, but with humility of mind regard one another as more important than yourselves; do not merely look out for your own personal interests, but also for the interests of others.*

The New English Translation *- Instead of being motivated by selfish ambition or vanity, each of you should, in humility, be moved to treat one another as more important than yourself. Each of you should be concerned not only about your own interests, but about the interests of others as well.*

- Vision members should not only possess ownership of the vision but be instilled with the ability to advance, maintain, and sustain the vision even as you move on in life or in death.

- The leaders and members of the vision should receive encouragement, teachings, and accolades from you as the visionary that strengthens them to go forth in their destiny and even release the vision that God has placed in them.
- Though vision members are assisting you with your vision, the position and work they are doing should reveal who they are in God and further advance them in their calling and relationship.

When vision members are empowered and advancing in who they were created to be, and have clear revelation of the vision, they are enthusiastic about God getting glory and in doing works for His kingdom.

- They will willingly be on time, attend meetings, ministry assignments and engagements and complete their assigned tasks without complaining and murmuring
- They will do unpleasant duties and the behind the scenes work
- They will be self-sacrificing and obedient to God for the sake of the vision
- They will go above and beyond in seeking God for greater clarity in how to invest in the vision progressing successfully
- They will invest and acquire the necessary training and knowledge to equip themselves as a vision member

- They will celebrate the vision in purity and will not give into jealousy or covetousness as the vision advances

As vision carriers, practice the following:
- Consistently compliment and show appreciation for vision members simply because they are who they are in life and in God.
- Compliment and assist vision members as needed when you see them striving to grow and advance in the ways of the Lord.
- Compliment vision members when they do a great job or minister well for God.
- Do not degrade or belittle vision members when they do not do well in a task, position, or personal walk and when they need correction. Provide constructive guidance and criticism that empowers them to do better the next time.
- Equip vision members with the necessary study guides, trainings, and knowledge to improve in areas where they need to grow and that can further empower the calling and vision on their lives.
- Take time to pray, prophecy, and impart into vision members personally and as a team.
- Have regular one on one meetings to personally impart into vision members and to show them that you are personally invested in them.
- Have regular fellowships just to have fun and to bless vision members aside from vision work.

- Support vision members in their personal and vision endeavors and offer assistance as necessary.
- Provide opportunities within the vision for vision members to be empowered in their personal destiny and life's vision.

If you are implementing the following practices above and someone is still lagging in being a sufficient part of the vision or in fulfilling their position within the vision, then it is probably a sign they are

- not to be a part of carrying the vision
- out of season as it relates to assisting with the vision
- maybe in the wrong position within the vision
- simply not ready for the responsibility of a vision member

The vision is about operating in a spirit of excellence so that God's will can be done in the earth. It is important to discern this while making the necessary adjustments to secure the purpose, fruit, growth and progress of the vision.

When And Where To Release The Vision

It is important to release the vision when and where God tells you. You may want to release the vision at a particular time or in a particular area, however, God may lead you to another season and area. Sometimes where God wants you to release the vision, may not be where you want to live or even be. He may tell you to release the vision in the poorest neighborhood in the city, yet you will look at the natural state of the community and feel the vision will not prosper or advance.

> *Genesis 12:1-5 - Now the Lord had said unto Abram, Get thee out of thy country, and from thy kindred, and from thy father's house, unto a land that I will shew thee: And I will make of thee a great nation, and I will bless thee, and make thy name great; and thou shalt be a blessing: And I will bless them that bless thee, and curse him that curseth thee: and in thee shall all families of the earth be blessed. So Abram departed, as the Lord had spoken unto him; and Lot went with him: and Abram was seventy and five years old when he departed out of Haran.*

God separated Abraham from His idolatrous ancestors and sought to bless the destiny and vision on his life. In order for Abraham's vision to flourish, he had to leave his present country and go where God was leading him. Abraham's obedience was a determinant for Abraham receiving the nation and blessings God had promised him.

When we are releasing a vision in a particular region or area we are actually building an altar for God's presence to be established.

> *Verse 7 - And the Lord appeared unto Abram, and said, Unto thy seed will I give this land: and there builded he an altar unto the Lord, who appeared unto him.*

God knows where His presence needs to be established within the earth. It is therefore important to be obedient to releasing the vision when and where He says and to seek Him for the reason He has chosen a particular sphere of influence.

For Abraham, the vision was for the purposes of purifying a people who worshipped Him and Him only. For you it could be for other reasons. Yet whatever the reason, the vision only flourishes when it is established when and where God desires.

Sometimes the vision is huge and you have release it in parts.

> *Genesis 13:14-18*
> *And the Lord said unto Abram, after that Lot was separated from him, Lift up now thine eyes, and look from the place where thou art northward, and southward, and eastward, and westward: For all the land which thou seest, to thee will I give it, and to thy seed for ever. And I will make thy seed as the dust of the earth: so that if a man can number the dust of the earth, then shall thy seed also be numbered. Arise, walk through the land in*

the length of it and in the breadth of it; for I will give it unto thee. Then Abram removed his tent, and came and dwelt in the plain of Mamre, which is in Hebron, and built there an altar unto the Lord.

The Lord promised to give Abram all the land and encouraged him to walk to length and breadth of it. Abram did not let the lust of the eyes over take him such that he would get ahead of himself and strive to establish the vision in every place God had promised him. Abram did as God desired by claiming his territory as he walked and took in the land, yet when it came to establish an altar he pitched a tent in the land of Mamre.

This is vital as often we want to immediately acquire all God is promising. Yet we do not have or possess the fortitude to release, build and sustain the promises and work that are connected to the vision. We have to release the vision in the manner God is requiring and allow the vision to unfold as we progress forward in destiny.

Another key we see with Abram is that God promised the vision and nation to him and his seed. I learned from my mentoring program with Apostle Jackie Green, Founder of the JGM-PrayerLife Enternational Institute, that visions are generational. I learned that

- The work of a vision must be established where it can live on throughout generations.
- We may not get to release all of the vision and must equip those who are a part of the

vision to progress it forward and continue
the work that we have planted.

Genesis 15:5-6 - *And he brought him forth abroad,
and said, look now toward heaven, and tell the stars,
if thou be able to number them: and he said unto him,
so shall thy seed be. And he believed in the Lord; and
he counted it to him for righteousness.*

God promised that the destiny and vision upon
Abram's life would be as big as the stars in the sky,
and we know from earlier scriptures God said that
His destiny vision would be forever. This meant he
would not live forever but the vision that he
planted would exist even throughout eternity.

Releasing The Vision Decree

1Corinthians 3:13-14 - Every man's work shall be made manifest: for the day shall declare it, because it shall be revealed by fire; and the fire shall try every man's work of what sort it is. If any man's work abide which he hath built thereupon, he shall receive a reward. If any man's work shall be burned, he shall suffer loss: but he himself shall be saved; yet so as by fire.

Proverbs 24:27 - Prepare your work outside; get everything ready for yourself in the field, and after that build your house.

Lord I thank you that you have made my destiny and life's vision plain and provided everything I need to work and build your house. I SHIFT into action and release the vision that is upon my life in the name of Jesus. I hear you for your timing and I spring forth. I hear you for your will and I arise and shine in the glory that is upon me (*Isaiah 60:1*). I do not hesitate! I do not delay! I do not make excuses! I do not fear! I do not worry! I do not prove or waste energy explaining to the ignorant, blind, or unsupportive what you are doing! I just trust you and spring up into your well of everlasting that propels me forward in my destiny and vision (*Numbers 27:17*).

I am excited about my release. I am excited about who I will touch and the glory that will edify your name. I am now becoming those things that was not (*Romans 4:17*). They now are. My work is manifesting for my prayers and spiritual calling is becoming tangible materialize manna in the earth.

Thank you for being a God of miracles, signs and wonders and for making me a miracle, sign and wonder to the world. Thank you for the boldness to release my destiny and life's vision.

Reclaiming The Vision Decree

There are times when situations, people, and/or devils seek to steal our destiny and vision. We may even have released them to these situations, people or devils, or started a work and never finished it so it is in limbo. During these instances, it is important to assert our God given authority of rightfully reclaiming our destinies and visions.

> *1Samuel 30:8 - The Amplified Version - And David inquired of the Lord, saying, Shall I pursue this troop? Shall I overtake them? The Lord answered him, Pursue, for you shall surely overtake them and without fail recover all.*

> *The Message Version - Then David prayed to God, "Shall I go after these raiders? Can I catch them?" The answer came, "Go after them! Yes, you'll catch them! Yes, you'll make the rescue!"*

> *Joel 2:25-28 - The Amplified Version - And the [threshing] floors shall be full of grain and the vats shall overflow with juice [of the grape] and oil. And I will restore or replace for you the years that the locust has eaten — the hopping locust, the stripping locust, and the crawling locust, my great army which I sent among you. And you shall eat in plenty and be satisfied and praise the name of the Lord, your God, Who has dealt wondrously with you. And my people shall never be put to shame.*

*And you shall know, understand, and realize that
I am in the midst of Israel and that I the Lord am
your God and there is none else. My people shall
never be put to shame. And afterward I will pour
out My Spirit upon all flesh; and your sons and
your daughters shall prophesy, your old men
shall dream dreams, your young men shall see
visions.*

The Message Version - *I'll make up for the
years of the locust, the great locust devastation--
Locusts savage, locusts deadly, fierce locusts,
locusts of doom, That great locust invasion I sent
your way. You'll eat your fill of good food.
You'll be full of praises to your God, The God
who has set you back on your heels in wonder.
Never again will my people be despised. You'll
know without question that I'm in the thick of life
with Israel, That I'm your God, yes, your God,
the one and only real God. Never again will my
people be despised. "And that's just the
beginning: After that--" I will pour out my
Spirit on every kind of people: Your sons will
prophesy, also your daughters. Your old men will
dream, your young men will see visions.*

In the name of Jesus, we reclaim the vision God has
granted to our hands. We rescue it from every
undesirable state, while commanding it to be
restored to its original - natural formation and
revelation. We recover every fashion of it in the
purity to which God gave it to us and bring back
the vision to God's preferable manner of livelihood,
soundness, sound principles, fruitful ideas, and
kingly condition. We command every uncultivated

and wasteland area of our vision to be regenerated and empowered even now in the name of Jesus.

We repent for every portion of the vision that we have given over to the enemy and reclaim ownership and full possession of it in the name of Jesus. We repent for fear, insecurity, stagnation, procrastination, and immature mishandling of the vision. We repent for anyway we did not seek the Lord's timing, operated in our own strength and intellect; thus exposing the vision to unnecessary warfare and the annihilating attack of the enemy.

We restore the years that the locust hath eaten, the cankerworm, and the caterpillar, and the palmerworm. We repent for actions ignorantly or unknowingly, and command every way we have been hustled, manipulated, conned, or swindled into relinquishing our vision into the wrong hands or the snare of the enemy.

We say the vision is ours - it belongs to me devil and you cannot have it. We take full responsibility of reclaiming, reestablishing, and reuniting with purpose and destiny of the vision. We prophesy that we will never again disconnect from the vision. We covenant with the inheritance of the vision and with the reason God ordained it to be a part of our lives and destiny.

Reviving The Vision Decree

Sometimes we may experience lack, famine, and even death that thwart our destiny and life's vision. Jesus' destiny and life's vision was actually to die so that we could be eternally resurrected in our relationship, citizenship, and authority in God (*John 3:16, John 10:10, Romans 8:11*). So sometimes death is part of our destiny and life's vision.

There are also instances where the vision just seems to die or words and deeds are done to cause the vision to die. There is no age, time span, or limitation on God and what is of Him. God however, is about life eternal. He is all about resurrection and living, and living a life of abundance. What we think is a hopeless end, is an opportunity for God to revive our destiny and vision.

> *Psalms 36:9 - The Amplified Version - For with You is the fountain of life; in Your light do we see light.*

> *New English Translation - Verse 9-10 - For you are the one who gives and sustains life. Extend your loyal love to your faithful followers, and vindicate the morally upright!*

> *John 10:17-18 - The Amplified Version - For this [reason] the Father loves Me, because I lay down My [own] life — to take it back again. No one takes it away from Me. On the contrary, I lay it down voluntarily. [I put it from Myself]. I am authorized and have power to lay it down (to*

resign it) and I am authorized and have power to take it back again. These are the instructions (orders) which I have received [as My charge] from My Father.

The Message Version - *This is why the Father loves me: because I freely lay down my life. And so I am free to take it up again. No one takes it from me. I lay it down of my own free will. I have the right to lay it down; I also have the right to take it up again. I received this authority personally from my Father. "*

Romans 8:11 – The Amplified Version - *And if the Spirit of Him Who raised up Jesus from the dead dwells in you, [then] He Who raised up Christ Jesus from the dead will also restore to life your mortal (short- lived, perishable) bodies through His Spirit Who dwells in you.*

Jesus just as you died on the cross and rose again, we say the vision is not dead. Our vision is filled with your resurrection life, exhilarating word and divine purpose. Our vision is being vindicated with your cascading light of life. Even as we assert vindication, we speak life into the vision and command a quickening to its very existence in the name of Jesus.

We activate the vision with fresh life, supernaturally set in motion a fresh start of its growth, production and reproduction, and restore to life and consciousness the very wealth of what God desires it to be and do. We renew it, revive it and declare it is operative or valid again. We bring it back into notice, use, currency, and prosperity.

We reanimate the very chemistry and heavenly DNA of its character and nature. We posture the vision before God's throne to be blessed and saturated with His glory for His glory.

We say the vision has been redeemed by the blood of the lamb and the reviving power of Jesus Christ. Revival come to the vision. Rebirthing come to the vision. A great resurgence of God's authority and competency overtakes the vision. We bless God that the fountain of life has been restored to the vision and that we have been reconciled to fight the good fight of faith in seeing it coming to pass.

Thank you God that no devil or person can kill the vision. You Lord have the keys to death and hell. You have authority to lay it down and authority to take it up again. We thank you for your desire and will to revive our vision.

Restoring The Vision

For insightful revelation on restoration read the parable of the prodigal son in *Luke 15:11-32*. This parable reveals to us that should we get out of alignment in relations to our destinies and visions, God is always eager to restore us and our life's vision. He is such a good God that He at times, will restore us to a greater state than what we were originally. I believe this is God's way of showing His excitement for our willingness to be reestablished in our rightful place in Him. He is also equipping us with the ability to sustain in our restored place.

> *Zechariah 9:12 - New International Version - Return to your fortress, O prisoners of hope; even now I announce that I will restore twice as much to you.*
>
> *The Amplified Version - Return to the stronghold [of security and prosperity], you prisoners of hope; even today do I declare that I will restore double your former prosperity to you.*
>
> *Job 42:10 - English Standard Version - And the Lord restored the fortunes of Job, when he had prayed for his friends. And the Lord gave Job twice as much as he had before.*

When God restores us, it is as if we are renewed again. The old is stripped away and all things become new. Returning to agreeable lines with Him seems to cleanse sins, mishaps, regrets, and we can start fresh in our relationship with Him, and with journeying in our destiny and life's vision.

> *2Corinthians 5:17 – English Standard Version - Therefore, if anyone is in Christ, he is a new creation. The old has passed away; behold, the new has come.*

> *Isaiah 61:7 - English Standard Version - Instead of your shame there shall be a double portion; instead of dishonor they shall rejoice in their lot; therefore in their land they shall possess a double portion; they shall have everlasting joy.*

I do believe that a key to being successfully restored is knowing where we erred and then realigning at that place. This requires us acknowledging that we sin and have disconnected our relationship and alignment with God and now we are in need of reconciliation and restoration. In our acknowledgment and willingness to humble ourselves before God, He rewards us in making a pathway fresh and new for us to operate in.

> *Hosea 6:1 - English Standard Version - Come, let us return to the Lord; for he has torn us, that he may heal us; he has struck us down, and he will bind us up.*

Sometimes restoration is tied to generational blessings. We are seeking God to restore what has been stolen from our family line. As we reclaim it, God restores it unto us, and we are able to see increased blessing when journeying in our destiny and life's vision.

Joel 2:23-26 – Be glad then, ye children of Zion, and rejoice in the Lord your God: for he hath given you the former rain moderately, and he will cause to come down for you the rain, the former rain, and the latter rain in the first month. And the floors shall be full of wheat, and the vats shall overflow with wine and oil. And I will restore to you the years that the locust hath eaten, the cankerworm, and the caterpiller, and the palmerworm, my great army which I sent among you. And ye shall eat in plenty, and be satisfied, and praise the name of the Lord your God, that hath dealt wondrously with you: and my people shall never be ashamed.

Restoring The Vision Decree

Even now Lord, we decree that every imprisoned vision is being restored to its original owner, lineage, and to its original intent rank and purpose. We decree it is being brought back into existence, use, and likeness. We decree every vision is being reestablished to its former, original, and normal condition to which God created it.

We decree that everything that has been torn, struck, discombobulated, bound and dismantled with the visionary and the vision is restored to order now in Jesus name. Let the visionary and vision's very foundation, state, structure, creativity, uniqueness, soundness, vigor, SHIFT into its former place, position, posture, rank in Jesus name. We decree the visions' return and restitution of anything that has been taken away or lost. We decree double the restoration and prosperity declared in *Zechariah 9:12*. We decree *Isaiah 61:7*, while asserting that instead of shame there shall be a double portion; instead of dishonor, the visionary shall rejoice in their lot. In our land and sphere and everywhere we release the vision, we shall possess a double portion; we shall have everlasting joy.

Lord even as you restored the fortunes of Job, you are forgiving us as visionaries, providing clarity concerning who you are, who we are as vision carriers and providing double restitution so that your will and glory can be established in the earth.

Thank you Lord for giving the early rain as vindication, for pouring down your abundant rain, the early, and the latter rain. Thank you Lord that the threshing floors of our visions shall be full of grain; the vats shall overflow with wine and oil. Thank you for restoring the years that the swarming locust has eaten, the hopper, the destroyer, and the cutter. Thank you Lord that the vision shall be furnished with plenty and all that shall partake of it shall be satisfied.

We praise your name Lord for you have dealt wondrously with us and have not withheld any good things from us or the vision as we walk uprightly before you.

Birthing The Vision

Isaiah 66:9 - Shall I bring to the birth, and not cause to bring forth? saith the Lord: shall I cause to bring forth, and shut the womb? saith thy God.

Dictionary.com defines *birthing* as:
1. An act or instance of being born
2. The act or process of bearing or bringing forth offspring; childbirth; parturition: a difficult birth.
3. Lineage; extraction; descent:
4. High or noble lineage
5. One's natural heritage
6. Any coming into existence; origin; beginning
7. Create, deliver, produce, travail; other synonyms - an act of God, a blessed event

Because we are a literal manifestation of our destiny and vision to the world, we will feel as if we are birthing - feel the birth pains as the destiny and vision of who we are is being birthed and revealed to the earth.

Ecclesiastes 3:9-11 - What profit hath he that worketh in that wherein he laboureth? I have seen the travail, which God hath given to the sons of men to be exercised in it. He hath made every thing beautiful in his time: also he hath set the world in their heart, so that no man can find out the work that God maketh from the beginning to the end.

<u>_Travail_ in the Hebrew is _inyan_ and means:</u>
To ado, i. e. (generally) employment or (specifically) an affair, business, travail, occupation, task, job

Now I have never naturally given birth yet, but from what I have heard and from what this passage of scripture reveals, being pregnant and even being in a place of travail and expectancy is exciting, however, birthing is not going to always feel good.

At times, it is going to hurt, be uncomfortable and agonizing.

These birthing pains are instilled in us and are a part of who we are, so we will experience them regardless to whether we acknowledge or walk in our destiny or life's vision (also see _Psalms 139:7-11_)

Jeremiah 1-5

- Before I formed thee in the belly (we come from a place of controversy and travail - we experience and conquer it before being revealed to the world)

- I knew thee (made you famous in my eyes and to the world while in the womb)

- And before thou camest forth out of the womb (the matrix - something that constitutes the place or point from which something else originates, takes form, or develops)

- I sanctified thee (sanctification has its own purification travailing process and to have it in the womb, in the place of travail, well help Lord)

- And I ordained thee a prophet unto the nations.

  <u>Ordained in the Hebrew is *natan* and some of the definitions of the word are:</u>
  To add, apply, appoint, ascribe, assign, avenge
  To be ((healed)), bestow, bring (forth, hither)
  To cast, cause, charge, come, commit, consider, count
  To cry, deliver (up), direct, distribute, do, doubtless, without fail
  To fasten, frame, weep, suffer

Does that sound like birthing to anyone else?

> **Jeremiah 29:11** - *For I know the thoughts that I think toward you, saith the Lord, thoughts of peace (peace, friendship of human relationships with God especially in covenant relationship), and not of evil, to give you an expected end.*

"Expected end????????" As in "to look forward to, regard as likely to happen, anticipate the occurrence or the coming of, anticipate the birth of?????"

Let us just take a Selah pause and breathe a moment...

If you are one called to birth out other people, other ministers and fivefold ministry offices and works, members of the body of Christ, or the younger generation, your travail may be all the more increased and can occur until they become who they are to be in God.

> *Galatians 4:19 - My little children, of whom I travail in birth again until Christ be formed in you, I desire to be present with you now, and to change my voice; for I stand in doubt of you.*

Even the world - the earth - creation itself, awaits our birthing.

> *Romans 8:19 - For the earnest expectation of the creature waiteth for the manifestation of the sons of God.*

New International Translation - For the creation waits in eager expectation for the children of God to be revealed.

It awaits our natural birth, then it awaits our spiritual birth.

> *The Message Version Verse 19-20 - The created world itself can hardly wait for what's coming next. Everything in creation is being more or less held back. God reins it in until both creation and all the creatures are ready and can be released at the same moment into the glorious times ahead. Meanwhile, the joyful anticipation deepens.* (WHEWWWW! I love that version of the scripture)

One of the revelations God gave me was when the angels were calling out to each other, "*Holy, holy, holy is the LORD of Heaven's Armies! The whole earth is filled with his glory!*" in *Isaiah 6:3*, that word "filled" in the Hebrew means multitudes, mass, handful of, the entire continent." This was not just literal glory, but the world was being filled with mankind. We are the literal glory being birthed and revealed in the earth. The angels were reverencing God one to another, for who we were and how we fill the earth with and for God's glory.

> **Isaiah 6:3** - *They were calling out to each other, "Holy, holy, holy is the LORD of Heaven's Armies! The whole earth is filled with his glory!"*

WHEWWWWWWWW!

We have to learn to be okay with travailing and the pains of birthing our destiny and life's vision. For the earth needs us and awaits in eager expectation of us. We are birthed (born) and then we birth (birth glory) in the earth for God.

The World Awaits Me Decree

Romans 8:19 - For the earnest expectation of the creature waiteth for the manifestation of the sons of God.

New International Translation - For the creation waits in eager expectation for the children of God to be revealed.

The Message Version Verse 19-20 - The created world itself can hardly wait for what's coming next. Everything in creation is being more or less held back. God reins it in until both creation and all the creatures are ready and can be released at the same moment into the glorious times ahead. Meanwhile, the joyful anticipation deepens. (WHEWWWW! I love that version of the scripture)

Isaiah 6:3 - They were calling out to each other, "Holy, holy, holy is the LORD of Heaven's Armies! The whole earth is filled with his glory!"

Lord we decree a disclosing of our destinies and life's visions. We manifest, appear, and command the curtains of our destiny to be pushed back, for to the world we declare that we are being revealed.

We stop hiding. We stop denying destiny and our callings. We stop acting like people cannot see or do not need your uniqueness in us or that the world is doing okay without what you have instilled in us. This is a lie Lord for your word says the world waits eagerly for it. The world is expecting us to with intense anticipation, anxiousness -persistent

116

perspiring desires to experience you in us. The anticipation deepens even now. God reigns inside the awakening of our revealing even now!

You created the world to expect us. You created us to expect the world. This is a working relationship that you orchestrated when you breathed all of creation into existence.

We come into agreement with this relationship even now. We embrace the necessity of blessing the world with our destiny and life's visions even now. We are the glory that the angels were discerning in the earth as they cried out in worship unto you, "holy, holy, holy, the earth is filled with your glory!" We SHIFT from a hidden concealment of glory to filling the earth with our destinies and life's callings so that through us, you can get glory!

HOLY! HOLY! HOLY! The earth expects who I am, as I am your glory!

Healing The Vision Decree
Psalms 51

Have mercy upon me, O God, according to thy lovingkindness: according unto the multitude of thy tender mercies blot out my transgressions. Wash me throughly from mine iniquity, and cleanse me from my sin. For I acknowledge my transgressions: and my sin is ever before me. Against thee, thee only, have I sinned, and done this evil in thy sight: that thou mightest be justified when thou speakest, and be clear when thou judgest.

Behold, I was shapen in iniquity; and in sin did my mother conceive me. Behold, thou desirest truth in the inward parts: and in the hidden part thou shalt make me to know wisdom. Purge me with hyssop, and I shall be clean: wash me, and I shall be whiter than snow. Make me to hear joy and gladness; that the bones which thou hast broken may rejoice.

Hide thy face from my sins, and blot out all mine iniquities. Create in me a clean heart, O God; and renew a right spirit within me. Cast me not away from thy presence; and take not thy holy spirit from me. Restore unto me the joy of thy salvation; and uphold me with thy free spirit.

Then will I teach transgressors thy ways; and sinners shall be converted unto thee. Deliver me from bloodguiltiness, O God, thou God of my salvation: and my tongue shall sing aloud of thy righteousness. O Lord, open thou my lips; and my mouth shall shew forth thy praise.

118

*For thou desirest not sacrifice; else would I give it: thou
delightest not in burnt offering. The sacrifices of God are
a broken spirit: a broken and a contrite heart, O God,
thou wilt not despise. Do good in thy good pleasure unto
Zion: build thou the walls of Jerusalem. Then shalt thou
be pleased with the sacrifices of righteousness, with burnt
offering and whole burnt offering: then shall they offer
bullocks upon thine altar.*

Lord we decree healing over and into our destinies
and life's vision in the name of Jesus. We use the
sword of the spirit to infiltrate the very foundation
of our destinies and visions, and gut out everything
that is not like you. Every plant that you did not
deposit in the vision and us as the visionary is being
plucked up in the name of Jesus (*Matthew 15:13*).
We decree seed and crop failure to every root and
declare it will never grow again in Jesus name. We
decree the blood of Jesus is saturating the vision
and cleansing all pollution, curses, disease, death,
debris, and chasing away every demon binding and
contaminating the vision.

As we repent and bow to you Jesus, we declare that
we are submitted under a broken and contrite
spirit. We accept a crushing to be submitted to our
destiny and life's vision and believe that through
this crushing, we are being delivered, healed and
set free in you.

We say uphold us in a free Spirit that signifies our
healing. We say use us in destiny and in our vision
to draw others to you and to heal others as this
shows forth and gives you glory. We say cleanse us
of all bloodguiltiness that comes from our everyday

lives, day to day situations and dealings related to the destinies and visions upon our lives. We know this will ensure nothing gets between us and you Lord. And that is how we want to live every second of our lives. Created in your clean heart, renewed in your Spirit and in right standings with you. We thank you even now for healing us unto wholeness.

Nuggets for Cleansing Your Destiny & Life's Vision

Consistently seek balanced deliverance and inner healing for you and your vision and live a lifestyle of deliverance and inner healing

Anything you need to know to heal the vision the Holy Spirit can tell you, even generational things that are hiding in your family line and could hinder your destiny and life's vision. Do not be afraid to ask the Holy Spirit and spend time seeking Him for answers

Ask God for dreams, revelations and strategies for breaking stubborn cycles, strongholds, and spirits and the keys he give you to get free. As I am going to sleep at night, I soak myself in the blood of Jesus and power of the Holy Ghost and I welcome God to commune with me in my dreams and sleep. I get the greatest revelation in my dreams and sleep.

Consistently soak yourself and the vision in the blood of Jesus and the miracle and healing power of God. You want the glory of the Lord to be tangible so you and your vision can be healthy and so signs and wonders consistently manifest through your destiny and life vision. Absorb and clothe yourself in Jesus' perfect blood and deliverance power.

Cultivate a lifestyle of keen discernment. This will help you discern distractions that come to steal your time, attention, strength, bring stress, afflictions and bondage. It will also help you discern seasons as it is important to know which season your destiny and life vision is in. Keen discernment will assist you with hearing God clearly for revelation, answers and strategies necessary to progress in destiny and your life's vision, and to discern spirits, flesh, people, atmospheres, and regions. Be careful what you let into your five senses as this is where you discern. Cleanse your senses and imagination daily

Take time to rest, and receive deliverance, and to heal self and the vision. Take sabbaticals, take vacations, take personal days to rest, enjoy life and refresh yourself and the vision. Take soaking moments throughout the day to cleanse your, refresh, and absorb the strength and glory of Jesus

One of the definitions of rest is "repose down" which means to lie at rest, to lie dead, to remain still or concealed

As we are diligent in pursuing such a place of rest and calmness, our spiritual and natural posture should literally appear as dead. Things should die in us just because we have been obedient to resting in God

If you are still working, thinking about working, of preparing to work, you are not resting. Dead people do not work, think or prepare to work. Dying in rest prostrates us a place to total submission where God has complete control of our total lives and faculties. In the place God delivers, heals, prepares and resurrects us for the next season of our destiny and journey.

Cleansing The Vision Decree

Continually cleansing yourself and the vision from weights and bondages will be necessary as you advance forward in establishing the work of the Lord.

> *Hebrews 12:1-3 - Therefore, since we are surrounded by so great a cloud of witnesses, let us also lay aside every weight, and sin which clings so closely, and let us run with endurance the race that is set before us, looking to Jesus, the founder and perfecter of our faith, who for the joy that was set before him endured the cross, despising the shame, and is seated at the right hand of the throne of God. Consider him who endured from sinners such hostility against himself, so that you may not grow weary or fainthearted.*

In the name of Jesus, we break the powers and release every weight and burden that has attached itself to us and the vision. We repent for any sins we have committed in our efforts to work our destiny and vision and cleanse ourselves and the vision with the blood of Jesus and power of the Holy Spirit. We decree we are being stripped now of every ungodly evil and every devil and demonic stronghold is being exposed, judged, and loosed from us and the vision in Jesus name. We cast off regret, shame, guilt and every other condemnation as it relates to operating in our destiny and completing the vision. We say distractions are not our lot, and we remain focused and grounded in perfecting ourselves in Jesus and trusting that His works on the cross and power and blessings we gained from His resurrection is perfecting our faith and providing us the endurance to press forward in fulfilling our destiny and life's vision. We break the power of weariness and faintheartedness.

We cleanse these negative attributes out of our souls, hearts, emotions, minds, thoughts, and bodies. We decree the refreshing of the Lord is encompassing us even now. We are being drenched in God's renewal and fresh stamina as vision carriers even now. We spend time soaking in the presence of God so we can absorb His cleansing further and declare that even as we are being consumed, the vision is being saturated in the purity and wholesomeness of the Lord Jesus Christ.

Destiny & Vision Repentance Decree
(By: Nina Cook)

Lord we repent for:
- Personal sins both knowingly and unknowingly
- Impurities
- Ungodly habits
- Ungodly behaviors
- Ungodly leanings and sinful tendencies
- Things that we have given ourselves over to
- Unrighteousness that we have allowed to have reign and rule within our members, bodies, and souls
- Mistreatment and destruction of our bodies both spiritually and naturally as the temples of God

Lord we ask for forgiveness personally and generationally and repent for
- Generational sins- sins in our bloodline, sins of our lineage
- Repent for sins all the way back to Adam and Eve that have caused a shifting in our destiny and purpose of our creation
- The sins of the church
- Division and disunity within your body
- Criticalness and ungodly judgment within your body
- Gossip, slander, backbiting, sending fiery darts, friendly fire, and all ungodly conversation
- Lack of love
- The misuse of leadership and position

- Misuse of gifts: misuse of discernment, knowledge, wisdom, counsel, prophecy, apostolic authority, preaching, teaching, and evangelism
- Not accepting all of the gifts given to your church; rejection of certain gifts
- Contamination and mixture of gifts
- Compromise with the world and personal, cultural, and societal values and morals
- Misuse of your word, adding and taking away from your word
- Misinterpretation of scripture

- Grieving the Holy Spirit
- Not acknowledging and ignoring the Holy Spirit
- We repent for not honoring the Holy Spirit as the head
- Quenching the freedom and flow Holy Spirit

We repent for the sins of our regions:

God we repent for things being done in our regions that are contrary to your word and law
- Religion
- Tradition
- Witchcraft
- Control
- Idolatry
- Disobedience
- Perversion

Lord we repent for the sins of the land, for ungodly politics in our community, region and nation. We repent for ungodly bloodshed, murder, abortion, and all manner of destiny death, destruction, and murder within the land.

We repent and ask forgiveness for self-denial-denial of our callings, denial of who God created us to be, denial of destiny, denial of our design, denial of things that God has spoken to us, and denial of God's will, purposes and wisdom.

We humble ourselves further Lord and repent for all self-sabotage and any way that we have operated in:
- Treason
- Vandalism
- Disruption
- Destruction
- Demolition
- Wreckage
- Mischief

Lord we repent for our underhand interference in your production and will and purposes in our lives.

We repent for:
- Undermining your word in our lives and our ordained destiny
- Self-rejection and any way that we have renounced our destiny
- Every self-induced resistance and hindrance
- Every conscious and unconscious agreement and alliance with the enemy
- Acknowledging and receiving the lies of the enemy and lies spoken to us through other people

- Words curses that we have spoken over ourselves, negativity, and witchcraft

We repent for harboring unforgiveness and bitterness against those who have sinned against us. We forgive those who have sinned against us, spoken against us and the will of God on our lives, and who have wronged and hurt us. We release them and ourselves of any obligation, bondage, and captivity that may be due to unforgiveness.

Forgive us Lord for:
- Selling our birthright, identity, and destiny
- Not accepting and embracing our destiny
- Not aligning with the destiny and vision that is on our lives
- Not properly governing our destiny and life's vision

We fall out of agreement with sin, stubbornness, and disobedience. We come into alignment with your perfect will and plans for our lives. We thank you that we are forgiven and for the blessing to forgive.

Deliverance From A Poverty Mindset

Psalms 90:17 - *And let the beauty of the LORD our God be upon us: and establish thou the work of our hands upon us; yea, the work of our hands establish thou it.*

The Message Version - *And let the loveliness of our Lord, our God, rest on us, confirming the work that we do. Oh, yes. Affirm the work that we do!*

Deuteronomy 8:27 - *The LORD shall open unto you his good treasure, the heaven to give the rain unto your land in its season, and to bless all the work of your hand: and you shall lend unto many nations, and you shall not borrow.*

1Corinthians 3:7 - *So neither the one who plants nor the one who waters is anything, but only God, who makes things grow.*

Psalms 37:23 - *The LORD makes firm the steps of the one who delights in him.*

Lord we reject a poverty mentality. We repent for anyway we are trying to be our own provider. We repent for not releasing the vision or following your directives because we are focused on what we do not have rather than trusting you to provide what we need for the vision.

We repent for anyway we have given into hustling tactics, scandalous behaviors, a poverty mindset or the world's ways, in effort to fund our destiny and life's vision. We repent for being idolatrous and prideful in thinking that we can fund the vision through natural means or our own means. The vision is a spiritual sculpturally orchestrated design, and requires your hands and methods to bring it to pass. We repent for exalting our fear, insecurity, worry, and stress above you as our Lord and savior - as Jehovah Jireh - our provider.

We repent for a poverty mentality where we will keep wasting money on carnal, insignificance, or monetary things, but will contend knowledge, wisdom, counsel, trainings, mentoring, products, are too much or we are in lack (false or convenient lack) when it comes to investing in the destiny and vision on our lives.

We ask for forgiveness and break poverty mentalities rooted in our culture and generations, and that have been passed down to us from family members who have not properly governed their finances, destinies or life visions. We break the power of ancient curses of greed and financial manipulation and repent for every way our ancestors have abused and misused their finances, destinies, and visions. We repent for paying tithes out of fear that you will curse us or that the enemy can wreak havoc on us, rather than SHIFTING to freely giving through the life and spirit of Jesus - giving through a cheerful heart - knowing that you only desire to prosper and bless us.

We ask for forgiveness Lord and cleanse our souls, hearts, minds, mindsets, and generations with your blood and truth that you will make the vision plain for us. That means you will make it clear to us and all the world. You Lord will materialize our destiny and life vision for us and is keenly aware of every dollar, means, method, connection, and door/pathway needed to bring your word to pass.

Lord your word says you will open unto us your good treasure, the heaven to give the rain unto your land in its season, and to bless all the works of our hand: and we shall lend unto many nations, and we shall not borrow. So we SHIFT to our appropriate place right now as vision carriers. We work as you require and ask you and thank you for opening up the good treasure of heavens rain unto us. We thank you for blessing the land you have given to us and for blessing the works of our hands. We thank you that we are lending unto many nations and are assisting others with releasing the destiny and vision that is in their lives. We thank you for your beauty and loveliness that is upon us, that is blessing us, and that is establishing us even now. Your presence and provision is affirming us and securing us. Your presence and provision is letting others know that we belong to you and delight in you. Thank you Ohhhhhh limitless God for all that you do to make sure your glory radiates abundantly in our lives (John 10:10).

Spirit Of Excellence

Daniel 6:3 - *Then this Daniel was preferred above the presidents and princes, because an excellent spirit was in him; and the king thought to set him over the whole realm.*

Psalms 138:8 - *The LORD will perfect that which concerneth me: thy mercy, O LORD, endureth for ever: forsake not the works of thine own hands.*

2Timothy 2:15 - *The Amplified Bible - Study and be eager and do your utmost to present yourself to God approved (tested by trial), a workman who has no cause to be ashamed, correctly analyzing and accurately dividing [rightly handling and skillfully teaching] the Word of Truth.*

Ecclesiastes 9:10 - *Whatsoever thy hand findeth to do, do it with thy might; for there is no work, nor device, nor knowledge, nor wisdom, in the grave, whither thou goest.*

Colossians 3:23-25 - *The Message Version - Work from the heart for your real Master, for God, confident that you'll get paid in full when you come into your inheritance. Keep in mind always that the ultimate Master you're serving is Christ. The sullen servant who does shoddy work will be held responsible. Being Christian doesn't cover up bad work.*

Lord you are not asking us to be perfect but you are asking us to submit to your perfect will and integral character so that you can perfect those things which concerns us.

Even now Lord we fall out of agreement with sloppy work, shoddy work, half done work, sluggish work, poor and low quality work, poorly created work, stagnant work, last minute work, stressed and worry produced work, work we copied or stole from someone else, incomplete work, undistinguished work, second class and second rate work, work that is not rooted in your truth and purity, work of no godly character and excellence, uninspired work, mediocre and dull work, and work that is not founded in your vision, purpose and will.

We stop making excuses for the reason we cannot or do not produce excellent work. We stop presenting work and acting like it should be accepted when it does not have your quality, nature, character or excellence. We stop waiting until the last minute for things we have had significant time to invest efficient production and excellence in. We stop getting upset at others for not receiving our poor work when we truly know we have not properly invested that which was necessary to produce your fruit.

We stop operating in a sense of entitlement and expecting people to pay for work and bless us for work we would not even invest our own money in. We stop expecting others to invest in our destiny and vision when we ourselves spend our finances on other things rather than saving and investing in our own vision. We stop overcharging people and trying to act like our actions are the Lord. We stop letting people pimp our gifts and not properly invest in our products and callings, while letting them hustle and short change us - not because we are to be a blessing to them, but because they use their familiarity with us to save a dollar. We stop using religion and tradition and the name of the Lord to make people feel bad about wanting to be paid for goods and services we know we would have to pay for in the world. We reject these slave and poverty mentalities. We reject the spirit of mammon and scandal that makes us sell out people and our own souls for a dollar. We SHIFT into alignment of blessing and being a blessing in a healthy manner and by your design.

We say even now that we SHIFT into properly governing our destiny and calling. We SHIFT into a spirit of excellence and declare we are of quality and produce quality work that is outstanding and extremely good.

We decree we are distinct, superb, brilliant, and great. The excellent Spirit of Daniel rest upon us and we reign in high merit and divine. We gain the favor of bosses, governors, kings, leaders, high ranking officials because the spirit of excellence we operate in opens doors and produces abundant favor and blessing for us.

We are humbled in our excellence as we reject haughtiness and a "know it all attitude." We recognize that we are just a measure of Christ and pull others up even as we successfully excel forward and higher. We speak to our hands and decree they are blessed.

We stop sabotaging our own destiny and vision by seeking and investing in fame and platform spirits - where we run after names and people - but will not invest in materials, conferences and trainings of those we may not know, but yet possess the revelation to transform and SHIFT us into deeper relationship, alignment, and destiny in God. We study to show ourselves approved by going to college, attending trainings and seminars, and investing our time in materials that you lead us to that further equip us in our destiny and calling.

We recognize that when we reject any part of our destiny and vision, we reject parts of you God. We embrace the entire vision and not just the parts we enjoy or like or think we do successfully. For we recognize that excellence is not about what we present in public but what we do behind the scenes as well. We decree our private worship will be made public by your hands as you make room for us through the excellency that is on our gifts and callings. We repent for this behavior and SHIFT into accepting and governing every facet of our destiny and vision. We thank you Lord for forsaking not the works of our hands and that because we work in an excellent spirit, everything that concerns us endures and produces your glory from now until eternity. We declare we possess your spirit of excellence.

Plowing & Warring For The Vision

Jeremiah 1:10 - *See, I have this day set thee over the nations and over the kingdoms, to root out, and to pull down, and to destroy, and to throw down, to build, and to plant.*

Dictionary.com defines *plow* as:
1. An agricultural implement used for cutting, lifting, turning over, and partly pulverizing soil.
2. Any of various implements resembling or suggesting this, as a kind of plane.
3. To clear or to turn up (soil) with a plow.
4. To make (a furrow) with a plow.
5. To forcefully move through something, to tear up, cut into, or make a furrow, groove, etc. in (a surface) with or as if with a plow.

We recognize from the definition that plowing our destiny and vision implies that there is a cultivation occurring. When we are plowing the vision we will have to dig up or stir things in the
- Land
- Atmosphere
- Heavenlies
- Community and/or Region
- Destiny
- Vision
- People
- Generations
- The demonic kingdom and even in Hell

As our plowing stirs, digs, tears, turns, and clears away, we will have to further toil and cultivate, and even war to assert authority over our destiny and

136

life' vision. When plowing we are to be dressed appropriately because the work is tedious. We have to be dressed for the weather, the bugs and animals, and to protect ourselves from the stirring and the backlash of the plow and the machinery of the plow itself. This will ensure that we do not become overtaken as we stand against the wiles that come from plowing.

> *Ephesians 6:11-13* - *Put on the whole armour of God, that ye may be able to stand against the wiles of the devil. For we wrestle not against flesh and blood, but against principalities, against powers, against the rulers of the darkness of this world, against spiritual wickedness in high places. Wherefore take unto you the whole armour of God, that ye may be able to withstand in the evil day, and having done all, to stand.*

Efficient plowing will enable us to discern if we are sowing properly or if we need to pluck up and cut down some things in our destiny and vision that are not producing fruit and harvest. Sometimes, we will have to be patient before plucking up and cutting down, plow some more, and then see if fruit manifests. We may have to plow for several seasons or even years before knowing if our vision is benefiting from what has been sown. We will have to be okay with the loss should we have to dig out, cut, or clear away what is not fruitful to the vision.

> *Luke 13:6-9* - *And He told them this parable: A certain man had a fig tree, planted in his vineyard, and he came looking for fruit on it, but*

did not find [any]. So he said to the vinedresser,
See here! For these three years I have come
looking for fruit on this fig tree and I find none.
Cut it down! Why should it continue also to use
up the ground [to deplete the soil, intercept the
sun, and take up room]? But he replied to him,
Leave it alone, sir, [just] this one more year,
till I dig around it and put manure [on the
soil]. Then perhaps it will bear fruit after
this; but if not, you can cut it down and out.

Purpose For Plowing:

- There is no way around birthing and plowing.

- You will have to birth and plow each area of the vision.

- You will have to kill stuff you birthed then rebirth and plow that area again.

- You will have to keep plowing so your ministry can remain fresh and cultivated in the momentum, season, and newness of a God.

- You will have to plow because the enemy or just natural circumstance stagnated your fruit, utilized or even stole your fruit and production and plowing is necessary to get the production of your destiny and life's vision flowing again.

- You will have to plow to continually maintain and sustain in what you have birthed, released and planted in the earth.

It is said that before Steve Jobs died, he had four years of plans of Apple products in the works. This man was already rich and had changed the game plan of the computer, phone, and electronic industry. He could have just sat on a beach somewhere and chilled with his feet up. But even as he had birthed, plowed and produced, he was further birthing, plowing and producing until even in his death, he still maintaining and sustaining in his destiny and life's vision.

Cultofmac.com speaks these words regarding Steve Jobs:
"Steve Jobs has passed on, but his legacy remains something that cannot fade. His influence at Apple will continue to be felt in the years to come, thanks largely to the fact that he personally oversaw plans for the next four years of products before his death."

Plowing For The Vision Decree

Lord I bless you. I lift you up. I magnify your most holy and sacred name. I declare your name in all the heavenlies and declare you are Lord over me and all that concerns me. You are Lord over my vision and destiny and are exalted in every area and fashion of who I am. You rule and own the world and are glorified, evident, and sovereignly reign among all the universe.

Even now I repent for any way I have sinned and have sown negative seeds into my destiny and vision. I accept forgiveness and release those who have hurt me and attempted to wreak havoc into my destiny and vision. I thank you for the weapon of forgiveness and release my right NOT to be ashamed, guilty, condemned, angry, resentful, or to retaliate. I come into agreement with the work of Jesus Christ through the cross and resurrection and declare freedom and liberation from all sins and bondages.

I thank you Lord that you desire me to prosper and be in good health even as my soul prospers. I feast on your bread of prosperity and declare fruitfulness to every good seed sown into my destiny and vision in the name of Jesus.

I take on the whole armor of God and declare the enemies of my destiny and vision are exposed, defeated and cast out of my sphere of influence in the name of Jesus. I war from my heavenly place as an heir and declare devils and all wickedness are under my feet. I claim authority over my

- Land
- Atmosphere
- Heavenlies
- Community and/or Region
- Destiny
- Vision
- People tied to my destiny and vision
- Generations
- The demonic kingdom and even Hell

Jesus even as I dig, stir, toil, turn, and clear away in cultivation of my destiny and vision, I declare that I am armored in your blood, power, clothing and light and am standing unharmed against the wiles of the enemy. I rebuke and reject, backlash, front lash, fiery darts, witchcraft, mental and psychic warfare, afflictions from the weather and attacks of the enemy. With the blood of Jesus, I eternally close all doors to the enemy due to stress, weariness, being battle fatigued, striving to survive, generational and community sin and curses, and any other legal or illegal way the enemy would attempt to attack me and the vision.

I plow as long as necessary. I stand armored conquering the wiles of the enemy as long as necessary. I am patient and sustained in knowing that He who has begun a good work in me shall complete it until the day of Jesus Christ (*Philippians 1:6*). I thank you even now for the peace to be able to dig up and cut down anything that does not produce fruit in me and in the vision. I am at peace with loss as even as old things pass away, I know that through you, all things shall become new

(*2Corinthians 5:17*). Thank you God for giving me the strategy and fortitude to plow and war for the vision.

Conquering Afflictions In Our Sphere

Though the revelation in this chapter may not be for everyone, it will explain some of the warfare, wickedness, and afflictions some endure as they pursue their destiny and life's vision.

Because we are establishing God's presence as an altar in the earth through our destinies and life's visions, we at times will encounter and even manifest the sicknesses and afflictions that are in that region or in our sphere of influence to which we are planting God's work. We may feel our experiences are because of sin or an attack, as these are very valid reasons for sicknesses and afflictions. But as we plant a work, we become a part of that ground or atmosphere where we toil. We are being set - rooted – established - in that ground and atmosphere. The prophet Jeremiah is a prime example of one chosen to endure and contend in this manner for the deliverance and healing of his afflicted/sick nation.

> *Jeremiah 1:10 - See, I have this day set thee over the nations and over the kingdoms, to root out, and to pull down, and to destroy, and to throw down, to build, and to plant.*

As Jeremiah walked in his call and life vision, while delivering the warnings and anger of the Lord, he would experience emotional and psychological warfare when hearing the anguish of the warning sounds that went forth and the response of those recognizing or even ignoring the warnings and judgment of God.

> *Jeremiah 4:18-19 The Amplified Version -*
> *Your ways and your doings have brought these*
> *things upon you. This is your calamity and doom;*
> *surely it is bitter, for surely it reaches your very*
> *heart! [It is not only the prophet but also the*
> *people who cry out in their thoughts] My*
> *anguish, my anguish! I writhe in pain! Oh, the*
> *walls of my heart! My heart is disquieted and*
> *throbs aloud within me; I cannot be silent! For I*
> *have heard the sound of the trumpet, the alarm of*
> *war.*

> *Verse 21 The Amplified Version - [O Lord]*
> *how long must I see the flag [marking the route*
> *for flight] and hear the sound of the trumpet*
> *[urging the people to flee for refuge]?*

> *Verse 31 - For I have heard a voice as of a woman*
> *in travail, and the anguish as of her that bringeth*
> *forth her first child, the voice of the daughter of*
> *Zion, that bewaileth herself, that spreadeth her*
> *hands, saying, Woe is me now! for my soul is*
> *wearied because of murderers.*

Jeremiah experienced the agony of what he had to fulfill through his destiny and life's vision as a prophet of God. Even in *verse 21*, he inquires with God as to how long will he be subject to hearing the very alarming warning and judgment that he had to release in the nation against the people. Releasing such a judgmental standard was hard to do and hard to hear, and Jeremiah wanted to know the reason he was being punished for sins he was not partaking in. How long was he going to have to endure the consequences that came from operating in the calling upon his life???? WHEWWWWWW! Help Lord.

Jeremiah's life's calling as a prophet was to experience this level of spiritual sensitivity and anguish. Jeremiah was called from the womb to operate in this dimension of destiny and life vision. He was just a child when God began to use him in this level of prophecy and warfare.

> *Jeremiah 1:4-7* - *Then the word of the Lord came unto me, saying, before I formed thee in the belly I knew thee; and before thou camest forth out of the womb I sanctified thee, and I ordained thee a prophet unto the nations. Then said I, Ah, Lord God! behold, I cannot speak: for I am a child. But the Lord said unto me, Say not, I am a child: for thou shalt go to all that I shall send thee, and whatsoever I command thee thou shalt speak.*

Jeremiah embraced his calling, yet he constantly felt God's grievous heart, while experiencing the physical and psychological effects of wickedness and the afflictions of the nation.

> *Jeremiah 6:10-14 – The Amplified Version -* *To whom shall I [Jeremiah] speak and give warning, that they may hear? Behold, their ears are uncircumcised [never brought into covenant with God or consecrated to His service], and they cannot hear or obey. Behold, the word of the Lord has become to them a reproach and the object of their scorn; they have no delight in it. Therefore I am full of the wrath of the Lord; I am weary of*

145

restraining it. I will pour it out on the children in the street and on the gathering of young men together; for even the husband with the wife will be taken, the aged with the very old.

And their houses will be turned over to others, their fields and their wives together; for I will stretch out My hand against the inhabitants of the land, says the Lord. For from the least of them even to the greatest of them, everyone is given to covetousness (to greed for unjust gain); and from the prophet even to the priest, everyone deals falsely. They have healed also the wound of the daughter of My people lightly and neglectfully, saying, Peace, peace, when there is no peace.

Jeremiah 8:21-22 *- For the brokenness of the daughter of my people I am broken; I mourn, dismay has taken hold of me. Is there no balm in Gilead? Is there no physician there? Why then has not the health of the daughter of my people been restored?*

Jeremiah 10:18-20 *- For thus says the LORD, "Behold, I am slinging out the inhabitants of the land at this time, and will cause them distress, that they may be found." Woe is me, because of my injury! My wound is incurable. But I said, "Truly this is a sickness, and I must bear it." My tent is destroyed, and all my ropes are broken; My sons have gone from me and are no more. There is no one to stretch out my tent again or to set up my curtains.*

In *Jeremiah 1:14-19* we see God telling Jeremiah what would occur as he was sent as a set prophet to root out the nation. God also encouraged Jeremiah to *gird* his loins. *Gird* insinuates *"a clothing, armor, preparation, an equipment."* *Gird* does not mean Jerimiah would avoid ailments and warfare. Jeremiah was to *gird* himself because he would experience great affliction and wickedness, physically, spiritually and emotionally.

> *Verse 14-19 Then the Lord said unto me, Out of the north an evil shall break forth upon all the inhabitants of the land. For, lo, I will call all the families of the kingdoms of the north, saith the Lord; and they shall come, and they shall set every one his throne at the entering of the gates of Jerusalem, and against all the walls thereof round about, and against all the cities of Judah. And I will utter my judgments against them touching all their wickedness, who have forsaken me, and have burned incense unto other gods, and worshipped the works of their own hands.*
>
> *Thou therefore gird up thy loins, and arise, and speak unto them all that I command thee: be not dismayed at their faces, lest I confound thee before them. For, behold, I have made thee this day a defenced city, and an iron pillar, and brasen walls against the whole land, against the kings of Judah, against the princes thereof, against the priests thereof, and against the people of the land. And they shall fight against thee; but they shall not prevail against thee; for I am with thee, saith the Lord, to deliver thee.*

Verse 18-19 - The Amplified Version - For I, behold, I have made you this day a fortified city and an iron pillar and bronze walls against the whole land — against the [successive] kings of Judah, against its princes, against its priests, and against the people of the land [giving you divine strength which no hostile power can overcome]. And they shall fight against you, but they shall not [finally] prevail against you, for I am with you, says the Lord, to deliver you.

God made Jeremiah's very destiny and life vision a defense against the entire nation. He was the wall that separated God from the people, their sins, idolatry, whoredoms, blatant vanity, their laws (kings and governments), and retched living. The entire nation – people, kings and governments, the impact and results of their sins – where fighting against Jeremiah. And though God said he would prevail and he would be delivered, God did not say that he would not experience the afflictions and wickedness of his destiny stance. At times we see Jeremiah asking God for healing and deliverance for the afflictions and wickedness he endured on behalf of the people and the nation.

Jeremiah 17:14 - Heal me, O Lord, and I shall be healed; save me, and I shall be saved, for you are my praise.

Because Jeremiah literally experienced the impact of his rivals' wickedness and affliction, God had to remind him that He was chosen and that God's thoughts towards Him were good and would bring about an expected end.

Jeremiah 29:11 - For I know the thoughts that I think toward you, saith the Lord, thoughts of peace, and not of evil, to give you an expected end.

Like Jeremiah, we can be very self-focused when we are afflicted for no reason of our own. We require validation that God is for us and is journeying with us in destiny.

Jeremiah 15:15-21 - [Jeremiah said] O Lord, You know and understand; [earnestly] remember me and visit me and avenge me on my persecutors. Take me not away [from joy or from life itself] in Your long-suffering [to my enemies]; know that for Your sake I suffer and bear reproach. Your words were found, and I ate them; and Your words were to me a joy and the rejoicing of my heart, for I am called by Your name, O Lord God of hosts.

I sat not in the assembly of those who make merry, nor did I rejoice; I sat alone because Your [powerful] hand was upon me, for You had filled me with indignation. Why is my pain perpetual and my wound incurable, refusing to be healed? Will you indeed be to me like a deceitful brook, like waters that fail and are uncertain? Therefore thus says the Lord [to Jeremiah]: If you return [and give up this mistaken tone of distrust and despair], then I will give you again a settled place of quiet and safety, and you will be My minister; and if you separate the precious from the vile [cleansing your own heart from unworthy and unwarranted suspicions concerning God's faithfulness], you shall be My mouthpiece. [But

*do not yield to them.] Let them return to you —
not you to [the people].*

*And I will make you to this people a fortified,
bronze wall; they will fight against you, but they
will not prevail over you, for I am with you to
save and deliver you, says the Lord. And I will
deliver you out of the hands of the wicked, and I
will redeem you out of the palms of the terrible
and ruthless tyrants.*

Though God's validation brings comfort, it may not
readily bring healing. This is because the healing is
needed in our sphere of influence, and until that is
healed, we as vision carriers may continually
experience the afflictions and wickedness of what
we have been destined to pluck up, bring down,
and root out. Our focus then has to be on the
promises God has released concerning our sphere.
Otherwise, we will spend our energy trying to
hopelessly and shamefully heal and free ourselves
from afflictions and bondages that are really not our
own and thus cannot be cured through personal
means. It is a work that has to be done in the land,
atmosphere and region, and until that is healed, we
will battle these afflictions and wickedness.

*Jeremiah 30:17 – For I will restore health unto
thee, and I will heal thee of thy wounds, saith the
LORD; because they called thee an Outcast,
saying, This is Zion, whom no man seeketh after.*

*Jeremiah 31:18 - I have surely heard Ephraim's
moaning: 'You disciplined me like an unruly calf,
and I have been disciplined. Restore me, and I
will return, because you are the LORD my God.*

150

Jeremiah 33:6 - Nevertheless, I will bring health and healing to it; I will heal my people and will let them enjoy abundant peace and security.

God has begun a good work in those of us who are called to this mandate of destiny and He will honor His word. We have to trust that the work we are doing is producing His will and fruit even if natural circumstances within our region does not show it yet.

In studying the whole book of Jeremiah, we will discern that God recognized that Jeremiah's call was tedious. God walked closely with Him through His entire life's vision. God provided Jeremiah with the words and plan to contend against the godless nation. Jeremiah was able to endure the trials of his destiny and life's vision because he had a pure and honest relationship with the Lord. When we become weary and afflicted, we must be like Jeremiah and be honest with God about how we feel. This will enable God to validate us, remind us of His word, comfort us, and bring seasons of relief.

Casting Out Destiny Killing Spirits

In the name of Jesus, we break all powers that hinder, thwart or murder our destiny. We rebuke every power, plot and plan of darkness and evil in Jesus name, and declare the power of Jesus is overriding and infusing our destiny even now in the name of Jesus.

We break every demonic hold in our lives, generations, churches, ministries, regions, and nations that is hindering our destiny from coming to pass.

We declare we have been called and destined and command every fashion of our existence to align and yield to the calling of God on our lives.

We rebuke, judge and cast out of our lives and sphere of influence, every destiny killing spirit.

We rebuke your roaming and wandering and contend our lives and generations are off limits to you.

We rebuke your striving to instill fear as you lay upon us when we are asleep at night and as you try to strangle and suffocate us in our sleep and dreams. Your reign of terror is exposed and thwarted in the name of Jesus.

Even as the angels are taking charge over us, we close up every gateway you have had to our lives by using the blood of Jesus and the fortress of God, and we declare no more to your terror in Jesus name.

We send you running from our midst in your own terror and turmoil. May you be snared in the trap that you meant for us!

Traditional and cultural spirits that keep us stuck and from pursuing the uniqueness of our destiny and life's vision, be bound and cast out of our lives and sphere of influence in the name of Jesus.

Procrastination, stagnation, spirit of excuse, entitlement and justification, we fall out of agreement with you and command you to loose your grip on our lives and generations in the name of Jesus.

Self-sabotage we expose you for the undermining devil you are and we say loose us. We get out of our own way and submit to the will and plan of God for our lives right now in the name of Jesus.

Spirits of lust, lust of the eyes and the prides of life, we declare you are evil and wicked and we dismantle your authority and wooings in our lives. We rebuke coveting and desiring the lives of others, wanting to be other people, wanting to fit into clicks and systems that are not of God, lusting after things, people, and material goods that do not please God.

We command our will and desires to come under the subjection of the Holy Spirit in us and we submit our flesh, thoughts and emotions to a lifestyle of prayer, fasting, studying, and living out God's word. We SHIFT to becoming the very nature and character of God.

We fall out of agreement with and cast down all spirits of idolatry, fornication, tempting Christ, murmuring, and complaining. We judge you and command you to be bound and cast out of us in the name of Jesus.

We say evil things loose us. We say ungodly spirits and endeavors loose us.

We break and cleanse every time released curse that is instilled in the heaven lies against us. We snuff out the demonic prophecies and command the stars and heavens to be cleansed concerning us through the power of the blood of Jesus.

We reject witchcraft and bewitchment and break spells of witches, warlocks, word curses and belittling and beguiling words of leaders, loved ones, and words that were spoken as a joke or to discourage and keep us bound.

We eternally wipe these words and curses off our souls, minds, emotions, and out of the atmosphere, and eternally annihilate and snuff out every demonic seed, fruit, and manifestation of them in the name of Jesus.

We say only what God has spoken about us is written on our souls, cultivated in our minds and emotions, and reside in the atmosphere, stars, heavenlies, and world around us.

We fall out of agreement with any spirits that will try to get us to sell our birthright or to sell out to the demonic realm.

Devil you are a liar. We expose your cunning and conniving acts right now in the name of Jesus. We rebuke and command your trickery to become your own mantle of shame even now in the name of Jesus.

We partner with God and cancel every demonic partnering in the name of Jesus. We reject demonic promotion and disallow any claim the enemy would attempt to have over our destiny.

It is the will of God that is exalting us. It is the will of God that is propelling us. It is the pleasure of God that is SHIFTING us into success and is releasing blessings and the fruit of the vision into our lives.

Reconstructing The Vision

Reconstruction is necessary when we need to revamp some areas of the vision that may not be working, are not beneficial to the vision or need rebuilding and reordering within the vision. Reconstruction does not necessarily mean failure, or punishment for mistakes or sins, it is a natural process and will be essential as the vision unfolds.

> *2Corinthians 5 :1-2 - For we know that if the earthly tent which is our house is torn down, we have a building from God, a house not made with hands, eternal in the heavens. For indeed in this house we groan, longing to be clothed with our dwelling from heaven*

> *1Peter 2:5 - You yourselves like living stones are being built up as a spiritual house, to be a holy priesthood, to offer spiritual sacrifices acceptable to God through Jesus Christ.*

> *Psalms 127:1 - Except the LORD build the house, they labour in vain that build it: except the LORD keep the city, the watchman waketh [but] in vain.*

Even in the natural when a building is built, repairs and reconstruction has to be done to maintain and sustain the building. There are instances where work is needed in the foundation of the building to further strengthen it in its ability to handle age, maturity, and use. This is no different in the spiritual realm or with our destinies and visions.

We must embrace reconstruction and know that we may have to revamp:

- People and positions
- The manner in which we complete tasks
- How we spend our finances
- How we equip those who are a part of our vision
- How we minister and impart into those who partake of our destiny and vision
- The entire vision plan itself (every year I visit and make changes to the vision as God is leading)

God is always moving and changing. He is progressive, so we must be progressive. We must resist building high places that become religions and traditions as God is about advancement, and what worked in one season may not work in the next season of the vision. Flow with God and reconstruct the vision by His design.

Reconstructing The Vision Decree

Lord we acknowledge you as Elohim our creator.
Our destinies and visions are not made with hands,
but are indeed formed and built by the creation of
the Almighty and All-Powerful One. Even now we
release the building, revamping, reordering and
reconstructing of our visions to you. We shift and
decree that the reconstruction of our visions are
being led, directed, and orchestrated by The Lord.
We are only harkening unto your guidance, plans,
blueprints and design for our destinies and visions
to unfold, prosper, flourish, and prevail.

We submit to you Lord and align with your will
and plans concerning our destinies and visions.
Wills align, desires align, plans align, mind align,
thoughts align, heart align; we command
everything within us and that pertains to us to align
with Gods will and construction for our destinies
and visions. Even now we command those who are
a part of the vision, affiliated with our vision, and
connected to our visions in any way to shift and
come into full order and alignment in the name of
Jesus. We declare you as the ultimate builder,
leader, and constructor of our visions.

We repent for ways we have ignored, and turned
away from your counsel and wisdom concerning
our destinies and visions and turned to our own
agendas. We repent for listening to and
implementing the ungodly counsel of others and
allowing our visions to become man made lacking
your nature, your purity, holiness, character,
definition, and design. We repent for meddling in

the Creators creation and operating in idolatry as if we are our own creator. We repent for the mindset that we can build on our own and do not need your guidance and structuring to bring our visions forth. We declare that our visions are like living stones being built up as a spiritual house to be a holy priesthood. Yes we declare our visions and destinies are a holy priesthood! And because of such, our destinies offer up spiritual sacrifices that bring you glory and are acceptable to you.

We renounce and fall out of agreement with the mindset that having to change things and reconstruct the vision means failure, punishment, or that we have sinned and been displeasing to God. We declare a cleansing out of our thoughts and visions in the blood of Jesus, and command the curses of these words to be broken and rendered powerless right now in the name of Jesus. We come to a place of peace and embrace the always moving, changing, and progressive nature of The Lord. We embrace reconstruction in the areas of people and positions, how we complete tasks, how we spend finances, how we minister and impart, and the entire vision as a whole. And command every high place, tradition, religion, and idolatrous structure to come down and out of our destinies and visions right now in the name of Jesus. We flow with God and are aligned with His structure and design.

We declare that our vision shall sustain, maintain, and consistently be strengthened. It is The Lord who builds and works through us and our labor will not be in vain, but will be fruitful. Our building (visions and destinies) are clothed with our eternal dwelling from heaven.

THY KINGDOM COME DECREE
(By: Brandie Reese)

Matthew 6:33 - But seek ye first the kingdom of God, and his righteousness; and all these things shall be added unto you.

Matthew 6:9-11 - After this manner therefore pray ye: Our Father which art in heaven, Hallowed be thy name. Thy kingdom come. Thy will be done in earth, as it is in heaven. Give us this day our daily bread.

Shake the heavens Oh God and fill our house with Your glory. Thunder in the heavens against the enemy, O Lord. Let the heavens drop at the presence of God. Let the heavens praise Thy wonders, O Lord.

Show your wonders in the heavens. Show your wonders in our destinies and visions. Ride upon the heavens and release your voice, O Lord. Release your manifold wisdom to the powers in the heavens. Your kingdom come your will be done on earth as it is in heaven!

We declare that Christ in us is the hope of glory - Show us your glory Lord.
Make all your goodness pass before us and proclaim before us YOUR name 'The Lord.' I AM WHO I AM! You are a matchless –sovereign God!

We exalt you we esteem you. We declare your glory over all the earth. We declare that you are ruling and reigning. We bow before you and your

161

glorious presence. We are consumed with your
glory as it fills the earth!

Your are the King of heaven
The Good shepherd
Majesty on high
Ultimate and only creator
Soul healer
Light giver
The destiny releaser
The vision giver
The destiny and vision provider
Heart revealer
Dream awakener
All mighty God
Convent keeper
Doer of wonders

We go from Glory to Glory in you! We shift higher
in you! Deeper realms of your glory! Heavy
weight glory begins to penetrate us, our destiny,
and our vision, right now in the name of Jesus!!!

We were created for greatness! We manifest your
glory through our obedience to you God! We
glorify you when we accomplish what you set out
for us. You called us to this gospel that you might
share in the glory of our Lord Jesus Christ.

We carry your glory! The same glory that you gave
Jesus you have given to us! We honor you! We
glorify you! If you are for us, who can be against
us, who can destroy our destiny? Our vision? You
are God and you will back us! You are for us Jesus!

No word from your mouth is a lie! We honor your
truth about us and our destiny and life's vision. It

163

is yea and Amen! A done deal in our lives and lineages.

We glorify you and honor you as we go forth with boldness to reach the destiny, vision, and dream that you have given to us. Lord you chose us that your fruit shall remain! Your glory shall remain forever! The fruit of your glory in us shall be evident.

You have called us by name. We are yours! No risen enemy shall abort your plans for us. Nor shall they abort your glory! Destiny is ours by the right and authority of Jesus! The vision is plain and established through the resurrection of Jesus and us being heirs to your throne.

Your glory is evident and tangible and is removing the scales off our eyes. Vision is coming forth in the name of Jesus. Eye gates are being cleansed and purified in the name of Jesus!

We thank you for angels that are being released to war against any spirit in the heavens assigned to block your kingdom from coming, your glory from manifesting and thank you that our prayers answered. We receive the rain and blessing from heaven upon our destinies and visions in Jesus name. Amen! Amen!

Drench The Vision in the Spirit of The Lord

Isaiah 58:11-12 - And the Lord shall guide thee continually, and satisfy thy soul in drought, and make fat thy bones: and thou shalt be like a watered garden, and like a spring of water, whose waters fail not. And they that shall be of thee shall build the old waste places: thou shalt raise up the foundations of many generations; and thou shalt be called, the repairer of the breach, the restorer of paths to dwell in.

Acts 2:17-18 - And it shall come to pass in the last days, saith God, I will pour out of My Spirit upon all flesh; and your sons and your daughters shall prophesy, and your young men shall see visions, and your old men shall dream dreams. And on my servants and on my handmaidens I will pour out in those days of my spirit and they shall prophesy.

Our destiny and life's visions manifest as God's pours out His Spirit and waters the giftings and callings that are upon our lives.

<u>*Out* is *cheo* in the Greek and means:</u>
1. To pour, to pour forth; figuratively, to bestow
2. Gush (pour) out, run greedily (out), shed (abroad, forth), spill
3. Shed, shed forth, spill, run out, run greedily, shed abroad
4. Metaphor: to bestow or distribute largely

Out suggests a continuous outpouring which allows our destiny and visions to consistently be drenched by the presence of God, while enabling them to grow and prosper. God guides us continuously through His outpouring, making sure every provision and need is met regarding our destiny and life vision. The destiny and calling upon our lives thus become continual prophecies that are fulfilling the word of God in the earth.

As our destinies and life's visions are cultivated by God's Spirit, they are able to produce the presence and kingdom of God in the earth. God's presence is what rest and cleaves upon us and allows us to create as we speak forth and activate what is inside of His Spirit.

> *Isaiah 11:2 – The Spirit of the Lord shall rest upon him, the spirit of wisdom and understanding, the spirit of counsel and might, the spirit of knowledge and of the fear of the Lord.*

> *Luke 4:18 - The Spirit of the Lord [is] upon me, because he hath anointed me to preach the gospel to the poor; he hath sent me to heal the brokenhearted, to preach deliverance to the captives, and recovering of sight to the blind, to set at liberty them that are bruised.*

> *Isaiah 59:21 - As for me, this is my covenant with them, saith the Lord; My spirit that is upon thee, and my words which I have put in thy mouth, shall not depart out of thy mouth, nor out of the mouth of thy seed, nor out of the mouth of thy seed's seed, saith the Lord, from henceforth and for ever.*

- Drench us with a heavenly soaking Jesus, make us your water log, your well watered garden.
- Soak us like liquid, passing through our pores, our loins, bathe the very depth of our existence. Bathe our destiny and our life vision. Outpour into what you have destined us to be.
- Wet us through and through as in a souse, steep; Oh douse us Lord.
- Cause your glory rain to saturate the rivers within us as you wash what needs to be cleansed out of us, out of our destiny and life's vision; as you drench us with what needs to incubate us.
- Impregnate, infiltrate, and infuse our lives, every fashion of our being such that we hold the greatest possible quantity of you.
- Oh God magnetize and charge us fully with your glory and the drenching rain of your Holy Spirit that empowers us.
- Consume us into a state in which no further increase in current is achievable in us, among us, around us.
- Marinate us with you until no more can be held or absorbed.
- Permeate Lord, suffuse us Lord; endow us Lord.
- Pervade us, charge us, inoculate us; fill us to the brim and overflowing.
- Saturate us beyond our demand of satisfaction. Saturate our destiny and life's vision until it feasts off the pleasures of your presence.
- Flood us, glut us, oversupply us, overload us, overwhelm us until you are sure we are your well watered garden; until it is evident that we are

drenched and enriched by your outpouring,
while producing your glory.

Groan Over The Vision

2Corinthians 5:4-5 - For while we are still in this tent, we groan under the burden and sigh deeply (weighed down, depressed, oppressed) — not that we want to put off the body (the clothing of the spirit), but rather that we would be further clothed, so that what is mortal (our dying body) may be swallowed up by life [after the resurrection]. Now He Who has fashioned us [preparing and making us fit] for this very thing is God, Who also has given us the [Holy] Spirit as a guarantee [of the fulfillment of His promise].

Romans 8:22 - And not only the creation, but we ourselves too, who have and enjoy the firstfruits of the [Holy] Spirit [a foretaste of the blissful things to come] groan inwardly as we wait for the redemption of our bodies [from sensuality and the grave, which will reveal] our adoption (our manifestation as God's sons).

Romans 8:26 - Likewise the Spirit also helpeth our infirmities: for we know not what we should pray for as we ought: but the Spirit itself maketh intercession for us with groanings which cannot be uttered. And he that searcheth the hearts knoweth what is the mind of the Spirit, because he maketh intercession for the saints according to the will of God.

Dictionary.com defines *groan* as:
1. A low, mournful sound uttered in pain or grief
2. A deep, inarticulate sound uttered in derision, disapproval, desire, etc.

3. A deep grating or creaking sound due to a sudden or continued overburdening, as with a great weight
4. To utter a deep, mournful sound expressive of pain or grief
5. To make a deep, inarticulate sound expressive of derision, disapproval, desire, etc.
6. To make a sound resembling a groan, resound harshly
7. To be overburdened or overloaded
8. To suffer greatly or lamentably, groaning under an intolerable burden.

As vision carriers our spirit will groan at different stages of the vision. We will groan for the following reasons:

- When we are birthing the vision
- When we are birthing different parts of the vision
- When we are SHIFTING to a new level within the vision
- When we are in intercession or at war in contending for the vision or a particular fashion of the vision
- When we are overburdened and overwhelmed and need to release the vision back to God

It is our Spirit that makes us aware that we are in a season of groaning. Our Spirit makes intercession for us with words of groaning that cannot be uttered with our natural language.

Groaning can feel like giving natural birth. Your emotions can be out of whack and you can be grouchy, emotional, antsy, impatient, and uneasy due to the anguish that comes from groaning. It is important to be aware of this so you can be cautious of your actions and govern your emotions properly.

The enemy would like to do nothing more than to abort what you may be birthing or interceding for so it is important to protect your Spirit when in a season of groaning. It may be beneficial to even enter a time of consecration to spend more time fasting and praying during this time. God can also release revelation to you regarding this season of groaning and how it impacts you and the vision.

Pressing To Fulfill The Vision

Sometimes, plowing the vision will be challenging and you will have to commit to pressing to fulfill your destiny and the vision.

> ***Philippians 3:13-14*** *- Brothers, I do not consider that I have made it my own. But one thing I do: forgetting what lies behind and straining forward to what lies ahead, I press on toward the goal for the prize of the upward call of God in Christ Jesus.*

Press in the Greek is *dio* and means:
1. To flee; to pursue (literally or figuratively); by implication, to persecute: — ensue, follow (after), given to, (suffer) persecute (- ion), press forward, suffer persecution
2. To make to run or flee, put to flight, drive away to run swiftly in order to catch a person or thing, to run after to press on
3. One who in a race runs swiftly to reach the goal to pursue (in a hostile manner) in any way whatever to harass, trouble, molest one
4. To persecute to be mistreated, suffer persecution on account of something
5. Without the idea of hostility, to run after, to pursue to seek after eagerly, earnestly endeavor to acquire

When you are pressing:

- You may be running to catch up or keep up with the momentum of your destiny and life's vision.

- You may feel as if your heart and soul are sweating blood and tears to maintain and holdfast in your destiny and vision.
- Negative thoughts may plague you as strive to stay in the momentum of your destiny and life's vision.

We see Jesus sweating blood in the garden of Gethsemane as He presses forward in the vision of sacrificing His life for us on the cross.

> *Luke 22:40-44 - And when he was at the place, he said unto them, Pray that ye enter not into temptation. And he was withdrawn from them about a stone's cast, and kneeled down, and prayed, Saying, Father, if thou be willing, remove this cup from me: nevertheless not my will, but thine, be done. And there appeared an angel unto him from heaven, strengthening him. And being in an agony he prayed more earnestly: and his sweat was as it were great drops of blood falling down to the ground.*

During these seasons, God will send natural and spiritual angels to strengthen you and even to help you press. As this encouragement is released to you, it will be important to release the negative thoughts to God and remain grounded in pressing forward with fulfilling what has been granted to your hands.

> *1Corinthians 9:24 - Do you not know that in a race all the runners run, but only one gets the prize? Run in such a way as to get the prize.*

Pressing Onward Decree

I decree that I maintain the momentum of my destiny and life's vision and press when necessary to be exactly where you are at all times Lord. I do not backslide or look backwards. I do not sway sideways or remain stagnant. I strain forward and do not allow my sweat and blood to distract me from the pressing that is necessary to do your will.

I thank you for the angels that you will send to strengthen me and even encourage myself in you when necessary. I do not just run the race, but I run in such a way that I achieve the prize. I thank you even now that the prize is rewarding and is producing in me an exceeding weight of glory (2Corinthians 4:17).

Strengthening The Vision Carrier

Philippians 4:13 I can do all things through him who strengthens me.

In the name of Jesus we decree that as vision carriers, we are mounting up all the more in the strength and diligence of God. We are sincerely realizing and enjoying all God is doing in us and through us - that He has developed us and equipped us for the journey and calling on our lives (*Hebrews 6:11*). We come out of agreement with unbelief, insecurity, worry, fear, and shift into completely trusting and having faith in God, the vision He has granted to our hands, and the strategies and plans He continuously releases to us to bring the vision into fullness (*Hebrews 11:1-2, Romans 1:17. Romans 3:28*). We embrace Holy Spirit as friend even now. We sacrifice our time and surrender self in a greater fashion, so that we can SHIFT into a more satisfying and fruitful relationship with our friend, the Holy Spirit (*Galatians 5:5-6*). We SHIFT into a love to pray, and a love to spend time in the presence of The Lord. Instead of worrying and fretting, we pray and fervently seek the peace and will of God for our lives and all that He has granted to our hands (*Philippians 4:6*).

Even as we SHIFT higher and deeper into a relationship and total alignment with God, we decree we wholeheartedly trust the word and promises of God. His word is a powerful sharp surgeon's scalpel, cutting through everything that attempts to hinder His will from coming to pass for our lives. Doubts, defenses, fears, confusion, and every other demonic, worldly, and soulish blockade is being cut into pieces as we lay open before God - humbled, eager to hear, and only wanting to please and obey His sayings (*Hebrews 4:12*). Insight come forth! Fresh revelation come forth! Clarity come forth! Words of Knowledge that transforms and saves lives come forth (*2Timothy 2:7*). New revealed mysteries of the kingdom of heaven come forth! We are drenched in revelation and strategy to revolutionize our lives and spheres of influence. We are equipped because we are submitted before God and transparent in purity and righteousness before Him.

Lord as vision carriers, we loose strength to our cohorts in this journey. We loose strength to the hidden vision carriers, to the exposed and wounded vision carrier, to the developing vision carrier, and to the vision carriers yet to be revealed. We loose strength to our brethren in general. We decree a divine link of unity is forming all over your kingdom and we are mounting up as a renewed army - steadying one another, bearing one another's burdens, empowering one another, and encouraging one another to never give up because you are not giving up on us (*Galatians 6:2-3, 1Corinthians 8:9-11*).

As vision carriers we decree our worship is being all the more liberated. We are prostrating all the more and are unexplainably abandoned, such that new wells and revelations of worship are being revealed to us. We are singing and dancing over everything, being grateful in our journey and

176

seeking reasons to praise and worship - sing praises of adoration and due glory unto our King Jesus. We open our mouths to complain yet praises bellow out of us. We open our mouths to curse yet blessings transcend us. The foundation of praise and worship within us flushes anything that would strive to agree with the enemy and the trials of this world. We are praisers. We are worshippers; in all we do we render King Jesus relentless glory. (*Ephesians 4:20, Hebrews 13:15, Philippians 4:6*).

We thank you even now Lord for knowledge, for the spirit of counsel and the eyes of our understanding being enlightened (*Ephesians 1:17*). We thank you even now for spiritual comprehension. We thank you even now that bewitchment and witchcraft are deactivated from our flesh, minds, generations and atmospheres. We repent for anyway we have used our gifts, callings and visions to bewitch others. We repent for any workings of the flesh of bewitchment, idolatry, self-exaltation, disobedience and rebellion. We expose our inner man and hidden motives to deliverance through the fire of the Holy Spirit and decree a fiery cleansing of every idolatrous and satanic attribute, manifestation and effect in the name of Jesus. (*Galatians 5:20, 2Peter 1:3-11, Galatians 5-22-23*). Restore us with your fruit and character Lord. Restore us with the purity of operating in raw untainted, uncontaminated power. Let us be set apart from the false ministers of this world through your fruit and character operating in us. And by all means, provide us with the ability to discern false teachers, false prophets and false apostles. We rebuke being swayed by false doctrines, a lukewarm gospel, and demonic voices and lights of the devil (1Timothy 6-3-5). We decree the ability to discern with keen judgment. We try every spirit and expose them with your truth oh God (1John 4:1-6).

As your vision carriers Lord, we arise in boldness that leaves a legacy of sanctification, consecration, and purity to the younger generation (*1Timothy 4:12, 1Timothy 6:11-12, 2Thessalonians 2:13-16*). We despise not our youth, but take everyday as an opportunity to get closer to you and for you to get glory out of our lives. All this we pray and thank you for the immediate signs and wonders that will follow this prayer. In Jesus name it is so, Amen! Amen!

Life & Purity Decree

Matthew 17:20 - *He said to them, Because of your little faith. For truly, I say to you, if you have faith like a grain of mustard seed, you will say to this mountain, 'Move from here to there,' and it will move, and nothing will be impossible for you."*

Philippians 4:8 – *Finally, brethren, whatsoever things are true, whatsoever things are honest, whatsoever things are just, whatsoever things are pure, whatsoever things are lovely, whatsoever things are of good report; if there be any virtue, and if there be any praise, think on these things.*

Lord we speak life and purity into our destinies and life visions. We declare life and that more abundantly to all that you grant to our hands and declare that we shall prosper exceedingly in everything that you lead us to do (*John 10:10*). We declare that our faith is immeasurable and we believe you for the impossible. We rely on your strength and eternal powers to maintain and sustain us in the vision. We stand in unwavering belief, with expectancy for all that you have said for us, and those who will partake in the destinies and callings upon our lives. We reject negative thoughts, doubt, impurity, contamination, lukewarmness, demonic thoughts, bewitchment, and alternate destinies and visions.

We meditate on you day and night, and cultivate pure thoughts about who we are in you and who you are in us (*Joshua 1:8*). We enmesh with

179

whatsoever is true, whatsoever is honorable, whatsoever is just, whatsoever is pure, whatsoever is lovely, and whatsoever is a good report regarding our destinies and visions. We decree your Spirit of excellence and virtue is upon us and our thoughts are healthy and wholesome. Through you God, we literally become these attributes. We are thinking your truths, absorbing them, and speaking them forth. They are life and purity to all that hear them and health to our bones (*Proverbs 3:8*). We say these attributes are worthy of praise because they are your nature and your character. We love what you love and hate what you hate (*Psalms 97:10*). And we love that your good report is about us and towards us (*Jeremiah 29:11*). You are our life and purity Lord so we consciously ruminate on you.

Trusting God Decree

Proverbs 3:5-6 - *Trust in the Lord with all your heart, and do not lean on your own understanding. In all your ways acknowledge him, and he will make straight your paths.*

Deuteronomy 1:30-32 - *The LORD your God, who is going before you, will fight for you, as he did for you in Egypt, before your very eyes, and in the desert. There you saw how the LORD your God carried you, as a father carries his son, all the way you went until you reached this place.*

2Samuel 7:28 - *O Sovereign LORD, you are God! Your words are trustworthy, and you have promised these good things to your servant.*

Psalms 9:10 - *Those who know your name will trust in you, for you, LORD, have never forsaken those who seek you.*

Psalms 13:5 - *But I trust in your unfailing love; my heart rejoices in your salvation.*

Psalm 20:7 - *Some trust in chariots and some in horses, but we trust in the name of the LORD our God.*

Psalm 25:1-3 - *To you, O LORD, I lift up my soul; in you I trust, O my God. Do not let me be put to shame, nor let my enemies triumph over me. No one whose hope is in you will ever be put to shame, but they will be put to shame who are treacherous without excuse.*

Psalm 28:7 - The LORD is my strength and my shield; my heart trusts in him, and I am helped. My heart leaps for joy and I will give thanks to him in song.

Psalm 31:14 - But I trust in you, O LORD; I say, "You are my God."

Lord you are our faith, our hope, and our reliance. You are the gospel truth in our destinies and visions, the anchor to which we place our stock. Lord you are our assurance, our confidence, our dependence. You Oh Lord are a surety for us. You are our strong conviction to which we entrust. We know our destinies and life's visions are a done deal with you. For you Lord are our guaranteed insurance, our affirmation, where we pledge honor, commitment, and covenant. We covenant with you in relationship and not what you do for us. But we thank you that in relationship with you, our promises are secure and your blessings are forevermore for us *(Psalms 16:11)*.

Lord we trust you to unfold our destinies and life visions with eternal achievement. Generational inheritance is our portion as we establish a lineage that worships, praises, honors, and lives in trusted relationship with you. We trust you to guide us as the lines of our lives fall upon pleasantly agreeable paths *(Psalm 16:6)*. We do not lean to our own strength or understanding, but remain grounded in your power and might. Oh how we acknowledge and journey in unity with you.

Every need is met because we are dependent on you. You ordained us for this calling from the womb, so you will provide everything needed for it to come to pass. We do not allow stress, worry, or fear to rule us in anyway. We do not give into hustling or demonic maneuverings and endeavors in order to meet needs. We operate in clear witty ideas and strategies because you are downloading revelation needed to fulfill our needs and desires. You are always communing with us, sharing with us, and revealing your will to us. Even in your silence we can trust that you are with us and for us. Yes we trust you Jesus.

We love to trust and hope in you Lord. What a privilege to have a solemn oath of faith in you Lord. We do not fear the future and give thought for tomorrow, for tomorrow will take care of itself (*Matthew 6:34*). We rest and work in the day and trust your sovereignty to bless us, lift us up, and progress us as we learn and walk in your ways. Thank you for the trusted bond you have with us. Thank you that we can relish and glory in trusting you.

Accountability Decree

James 4:13-15 - *Come now, you who say, "Today or tomorrow we will go into such and such a town and spend a year there and trade and make a profit" — yet you do not know what tomorrow will bring. What is your life? For you are a mist that appears for a little time and then vanishes. Instead you ought to say, "If the Lord wills, we will live and do this or that."*

Ecclesiastes 5:3 - The Amplified - *For a dream comes with much business and painful effort, and a fool's voice with many words.*

In the name of Jesus, I rebuke the spirit of the waster, distraction, seduction, and lust as these are spiritual cancers to my destiny and vision. I do not receive any sickness, affliction, and wooing that would draw me away from my destiny and vision. I remain fervent, while taking my destiny and life's vision very seriously.

I understand that my dream comes with much business and painful efforts. I understand *Romans 8:18* and reckoned that "the sufferings of this present time are not worthy to be compared with the glory which shall be revealed in me." I decree unexplainable glory will be revealed in me and the vision, for I pursue to do the will of God and position myself such that His manifest glory will limitlessly spill out of my destiny and life's vision.

I declare that I seek to dwell in the Lord's house and in His will from now to eternity (*Psalms 27:4*).

I declare I am a hard worker and God blesses and establishes the works of my hands (*Psalms 70:19*).

For if I live, I live for the Lord, or if I die, I die for the Lord; therefore whether I live or die, I am the Lord's (*Romans 4:18*).

To you Lord, I am accountable.

Visionary Rewards Decree

As you build and plow the vision, resist focusing on and seeking immediate rewards. Contend rather for eternal visionary rewards.

> *Isaiah 55:2 - Why spend money on what is not bread, and your labor on what does not satisfy? Listen, listen to me, and eat what is good, and you will delight in the richest of fare.*

> *John 4:14 - But whoever drinks the water I give them will never thirst. Indeed, the water I give them will become in them a spring of water welling up to eternal life.*

Sometimes when we are focused on temporary rewards we will take that as we are complete in the work of the vision, and we cease plowing and maintaining our destiny and vision the way we should. Or we take our eyes off the full vision and start to focus on how we can personally benefit from the vision. This is dangerous as we can get off track and begin seeking rewards and become driven by gain rather than by the will and plan of God. And when the rewards cease, we resort to implementing our own plan to maintain the worldly desires and lustful appetites we have cultivated within ourselves and the vision.

> *John 6:27 The Amplified Version - Stop toiling and doing and producing for the food that perishes and decomposes [in the using], but strive and work and produce rather for the [lasting] food which endures [continually] unto life eternal; the*

Son of Man will give (furnish) you that, for God the Father has authorized and certified Him and put His seal of endorsement upon Him.

The Message Version - *Don't waste your energy striving for perishable food like that. Work for the food that sticks with you, food that nourishes your lasting life, food the Son of Man provides. He and what he does are guaranteed by God the Father to last.*

Such a drawing away can hinder our destiny and life's vision. It can also sway us into deception as because we are gaining monetary things, we assume God is with us. Yet because we are not working our own destiny and vision, God is far from us.

Matthew 6:33-34 - *But seek ye first the kingdom of God, and his righteousness; and all these things shall be added unto you. Take therefore no thought for the morrow: for the morrow shall take thought for the things of itself. Sufficient unto the day is the evil thereof.*

The Message Version - *Steep your life in God-reality, God-initiative, God-provisions. Don't worry about missing out. You'll find all your everyday human concerns will be met. Give your entire attention to what God is doing right now, and don't get worked up about what may or may not happen tomorrow. God will help you deal with whatever hard things come up when the time comes.*

187

Keep your focus on God and His kingdom and if you are weary and need God to bless you, do not seek rewards yourself. Ask God to release them to you.

> *Proverbs 11:25 - The liberal soul shall be made fat: and he that watereth shall be watered also himself.*

> *Matthew 7:11 - ye then, being evil, know how to give good gifts unto your children, how much more shall your Father which is in heaven give good things to them that ask him?*

> *Psalms 84:11 - For the LORD God is a sun and shield; the LORD bestows favor and honor; no good thing does he withhold from those whose walk is blameless.*

> *Romans 8:32 - He who did not spare his own Son, but gave him up for us all--how will he not also, along with him, graciously give us all things?*

> *Matthew 7:7-8 - Ask, and it shall be given you; seek, and ye shall find; knock, and it shall be opened unto you: For everyone who asks receives; the one who seeks finds; and to the one who knocks, the door will be opened.*

Kingdom Rewards Decree

Lord thank you that you do not withhold good gifts from your children. Thank you that you care about how I feel, have my best interest at heart, and possess a desire to bless me. Even as I seek you first and your kingdom, I thank you that everything else is added unto me. I thank you that every need is met in my personal life and in the vision, and that you are sparing nothing from me.

I reject seeking rewards, prosperity, fame, and anything else that would separate me from you. I reject implementing my own plan for personal gain and vow to stay rooted and grounded in establishing your kingdom and building the vision of your altar that you have put in me. I nourish and feast off of the eternal weights of your glory and am sustained in your goodness.

I taste you even now and declare you are good God (*Psalms 34:8*).

I partake of you even now and declare you are good God.

I feast in you even now and declare you are good God.

Your word says you are able to do exceedingly and abundantly beyond anything I can ask or think (*Ephesians 3:20*). I therefore, fall out of agreement with the lie that I cannot ask or expect you to bless me. I reject the religious mindset that I am called to only be persecuted and not be blessed by your goodness. I assert my right as your child and kingdom heir to ask, knock and seek you for my needs and desires and thank you for answering my prayers.

Resting The Vision Carrier & The Vision

Ecclesiastes 3:1-9
To every thing there is a season, and a time to
every purpose under the heaven: A time to be
born, and a time to die; a time to plant, and a time
to pluck up that which is planted; A time to kill,
and a time to heal; a time to break down, and a
time to build up; A time to weep, and a time to
laugh; a time to mourn, and a time to dance;

A time to cast away stones, and a time to gather
stones together; a time to embrace, and a time to
refrain from embracing; A time to get, and a time
to lose; a time to keep, and a time to cast away; A
time to rend, and a time to sew; a time to keep
silence, and a time to speak; A time to love, and a
time to hate; a time of war, and a time of peace.
What profit hath he that worketh in that wherein
he laboureth?

We discern here that resting the vision is just as
important as working the vision. Often we strive to
avoid certain seasons. This is good if these seasons
are not of God. Yet some seasons are inevitable and
are part of the process of life and of maturing the
vision. Each season of our destiny and vision is
essential to its growth, success, and ability to
sustain throughout generations. If we are plowing
the vision by God's design, then we can trust the
vision to sustain and weather every season (*Psalms
1:3*). And we can be at peace with resting and
believing the vision will still flourish as it is settling
in the work God has led us to do.

191

All houses eventually settle. How the houses settle determines how stable and accurate the foundation was laid. If the house settles and the foundations begin to crack, this lets the home owner know that there were areas within the soil and laying of foundational concrete that were uneven or imbalanced. The house will manifest cracks that require attention so that the problem will not become worse, risking the house totally collapsing.

When the vision enters a place of rest, it settles and exposes cracks in the foundation that need to be repaired and healed. At times, when we are working a vision, it is difficult to discern where repair and healing of a vision is needed. However, when the vision enters a place of rest, the stillness of settling allows the vision to absorb the work that has been put into the vision, thus exposing areas that still need work and mending.

Many visionaries and their assistants are overworked, stuck, weary, dying early, and even aborting the vision because they have not taken their seasons of rest. The false obligations to be everything and do everything steals seasons of rest, then the visionary and even the vision collapses because there has not been a time to of settling where cracks can be exposed and healed.

> *John 7:8-9 - You go up to the feast. I am not going up to this feast, for my time has not yet fully come. After saying this, he remained in Galilee.*

Hebrews 4:11 - *Let us labour therefore to enter into that rest, lest any - man fall after the same example of unbelief.*

<u>Labour is *spoudazo* in the Greek and means:</u>
1. Seed (used in sowing): to use speed, i. e. to make effort, be prompt or earnest
2. So (give) diligence, be diligent (forward), endeavor, labour, study
3. Be forward, labour, study, to hasten, make haste, to exert one's self

The Greek word for *labour* denotes that when we are diligent to enter a place of rest in God, it is seed used for sowing. We sow in being diligent to rest, and God rewards us by doing or leading us in doing all the work that needs to be done in us and for us. We are totally submitted to His strength and His Spirit and do nothing of and in our own accord.

It is therefore important to have a passion in staying in this place when God is requiring it of us. We are to pursue it with passion as we would pursue anything that we deem important. We are also to be okay with ceasing from works, personal pulls, and pulls of people or obligations and responsibilities that will only drain and steal our time of renewal in God.

<u>Rest is *katapausis* in the Greek and means:</u>
1. Reposing down, i. e. (by Hebraism) abode
2. A putting to rest calming of the winds, a resting place
3. Metaphor: the heavenly blessedness in which God dwells, and of which he has promised to

193

make persevering believers in Christ partakers after the toils and trials of life on earth are ended.

Dictionary.com defines *repose* as:
1. To lie at rest
2. To lie dead <reposing in state>
3. To remain still or concealed
4. To take a rest, rely
5. To rest for support, lie

As we are diligent in pursuing such a place of rest and calmness, our spiritual and natural posture should literally appear as dead. Also things should die in us just because we have been obedient to resting in God.

Repose suggests that this rest should be as a death. The quietness we enter should be in such submission that we appear dead from doing works and totally submitted and focused in being humbled, bowed, and prostrate before Jesus.

> *The New Living Translation of Hebrews 4:12 says:*
> *For the word of God is living and active and sharper than any double- edged sword, piercing even to the point of dividing soul from spirit, and joints from marrow; it is able to judge the desires and thoughts of the heart. And no creature is hidden from God, but everything is naked and exposed to the eyes of him to whom we must render an account.*

This asserts that we are not trying to hide our sins and faults but are taking them to God - before him. As we are diligent in resting, His word goes in and surgically removes everything that is not like Him. It divides the good from the bad and cleanses us (our souls), while renewing and reconnecting us (our spirits) in places that were disconnected from Him.

The Message Version of Verse 12

God means what he says. What he says goes. His powerful Word is sharp as a surgeon's scalpel, cutting through everything, whether doubt or defense, laying us open to listen and obey. Nothing and no one is impervious to God's Word. We can't get away from it—no matter what.

The Amplified Versions of Verse 11-12

Let us therefore be zealous and exert ourselves and strive diligently to enter that rest [of God, to know and experience it for ourselves], that no one may fall or perish by the same kind of unbelief and disobedience [into which those in the wilderness fell]. For the Word that God speaks is alive and full of power [making it active, operative, energizing, and effective]; it is sharper than any two- edged sword, penetrating to the dividing line of the breath of life (soul) and [the immortal] spirit, and of joints and marrow [of the deepest parts of our nature], exposing and sifting and analyzing and judging the very thoughts and purposes of the heart.

195

Sharper is _tomoteros_ in the Greek and means:
1. comparative of a derivative of the primary _temno_
   (to cut; more comprehensive or decisive than, as
   if by a single stroke whereas that implies
   repeated blows, like hacking)
2. more keen, sharper

Resting Decree

We diligently seek to rest in you God. We repent for anyway we have not rested when you required it and we shift to diligently pursuing a resting place of refuge in you. As we rest Lord, let your word take refuge in us. Go deep in releasing your word in us Lord.

Let the sharp scalpel of your word surgically work in us Jesus! We willingly come to the operation table of rest to be judged by your word, to be delivered by your word, to be healed by your word, to be revived by your word, to be renewed by your word, to be refreshed by your word, and to be further directed by your word.

Lord, divide and separate us from everything that is not like you. Disconnect and gut out everything that does not look like or portray you. Penetrate deeply - pierce deeply where we are gutted out to the very foundation of our existence.

Everything that cannot go into the next season, we say scalpel it out Father. Let the sword be keen in discerning and removing all evil, all the demonic, and every crevice and fashion of the devil and his existence.

And as you do a complete work in us, as we die in you. Conceal your likeness in us Jesus. Reconnect us to you in places we have been detached. Reconnect us in places where we have been damaged due to past warfare, sin, or illegal violations of the enemy.

197

Ohhhhh!!! We die in you and rise in you Jesus. We die on your operation table of rest and rise into resurrection newness in you Jesus.

Yes! Yes! Yes! We take our rest and let you do you in us Jesus. We submit to the work that only you can do in this time of dying in your secret place of rest.

Expand The Vision

Isaiah 54:2 - *Enlarge the place of your tent, and let the curtains of your habitations be stretched out; do not hold back; lengthen your cords and strengthen your stakes.*

Lord I place no limits on the destiny and vision you have given me. For even as you are a huge and exalted God, and cannot be contained, I decree into the vision that it is forever increasing and prospering and advancing. I decree the tent of my destiny and life's vision is enlarging, stretching abroad, and being lengthened immeasurably. Nothing is holding back the vision as it is being strengthened by your presence and power on every side. I thank you that there are no barriers to the vision and that it will live throughout eternity. I thank you for a blessed and successful spiritual and natural lineage that will carry the vision onward. I decree they will remain pure in worship and relationship with you as you propel them and the vision forward in greatness that will be awe striking to all those who witness and partake of the vision. Be glorified and honored as only you can, in Jesus name, I am thankful and honored. Amen! Amen!

<u>References:</u>

The Holy Bible in different versions
Dictionary.com
Merriam Webster's Online Dictionary
Strong's Concordance

Cover Design and Layout:

Book Picture Cover is by Latasha Hyatt and layout
design by Reenita Keys
Connect with them via Facebook

Kingdom Shifters Books & Apparel
Available at Kingdomshifters.com

BOOKS FOR EVERYONE

Healing The Wounded Leader

Kingdom Shifters Decree That Thang

There Is An App For That

Kingdom Watchman Builder On the Wall

Embodiment Of A Kingdom Watchman
Releasing The Vision

Dismantling Homosexuality Handbook
Feasting In His Presence

Kingdom Heirs Decree That Thing

Let There Be Sight

Atmosphere Changers (Weaponry)

BOOKS FOR DANCERS

Dancers! Dancers! Decree That Thang

Spirits That Attack Dance Ministers & Ministries

TEE SHIRTS

Kingdom Shifters Tee Shirt

Let The Fruit Speak Tee
Shirt

Shirt

Releasing The Vision Tee Shirt
Shirt

Kingdom Perspective Tee

Stand in Position Tee Shirt

No Defense Tee Shirt

My God Rules Like A Boss Tee Shirt

Destiny Blueprint Tee Shirt

CD'S

Decree That Thing CD

Kingdom Heirs Decree That Thing CD

Teachings & Worship CD's

www.ingramcontent.com/pod-product-compliance
Lightning Source LLC
Chambersburg PA
CBHW051826090426
42736CB00011B/1666